NO TIME TO COOK

Copyright © Donna Hay 2008. Design copyright © Donna Hay 2008
Photographs copyright © Con Poulos 2008
Styling: Donna Hay
Art direction and design: Clare Stephens
Copy Editor: Kirsty McKenzie
Recipe testing: Ali Irvine and Hannah Dodds
Consulting Art Director: Sarah Kavanagh
Consulting Editor: Steve deVille

Reproduction by Graphic Print Group, South Australia
Produced in Hong Kong by Phoenix Offset on 157gsm Chinese Matt Art
Printed in China
09 10 11 10 9 8 7 6 5 4 3

FOURTH ESTATE
An imprint of HarperCollins*Publishers*

First published in Australia and New Zealand in 2008, by Fourth Estate,
an imprint of HarperCollins*Publishers*

HarperCollins*Publishers* Australia Pty Limited, 25 Ryde Road, Pymble, Sydney, NSW 2073, Australia
ABN 36 009 913 517
HarperCollins*Publishers*, 31 View Road, Glenfield, Auckland 10, New Zealand

NATIONAL LIBRARY OF AUSTRALIA CATALOGUING-IN-PUBLICATION DATA
Hay, Donna. No Time to Cook / Donna Hay. 1st ed. ISBN 978 0 7322 8816 7 (pbk.) Includes index.
Dinners and dining. Quick and easy cookery. 641.54

ON THE COVER
zucchini and mint pasta, page 112

donna hay

no time to cook

photography by con poulos

FOURTH ESTATE

CONTENTS

When I first contemplated starting a family, I imagined not much would change in my life. I dismissed as alarmist rubbish any suggestion that I'd find myself heading off to work a sleep-deprived zombie and returning home in the evenings with barely the energy to read a story book let alone prepare dinner. With the 20/20 vision of hindsight, I now know that I was being a tad optimistic and that all parents are legends.

Like everyone else these days work just gets busier and now that my husband and I have two small boys competing for our attention, finding time to spend with family and friends is more challenging than ever. Yet sharing meals is one of the cornerstones of our family's existence and we try to keep at least part of our weekends free for the very enjoyable business of entertaining.

With very little time for preparation and even less for cleaning up afterwards, the idea for *no time to cook* was born. And so it is that these recipes were devised as much for us as for you. For all the time-poor people out there, I've revisited my trusty old favourites, made some new discoveries, and even included some dishes that can be made in advance and frozen. I hope this new cookbook is one that you'll keep turning to time and time again.

Donna

ASSEMBLED DINNER

There are times when life is simply too short to cook. If the thought of a load of chopping, peeling and dicing makes you feel tired all over, it's time for a quick trip to the deli and your favourite greengrocer. Team your purchases with a savvy selection of snapping fresh produce and in a matter of minutes you'll be enjoying delicious alternatives to takeaway.

TUNA & HUMMUS DINNER BRUSCHETTA

VEGETABLE ANTIPASTI COUSCOUS

tuna & hummus dinner bruschetta

4 slices bread
olive oil, for brushing
1 clove garlic, halved
¾ cup (200g) store-bought hummus
40g baby English spinach or rocket (arugula) leaves
2 tomatoes, sliced
¼ cup mint leaves
425g can tuna, drained
2 tablespoons salted capers, rinsed
sea salt and cracked black pepper
1 lemon, halved

Toast the bread in a toaster or grill until golden. Brush with olive oil and rub with garlic. Spread the toast with hummus and top with spinach, tomato, mint, tuna and capers. Divide between serving plates, sprinkle with salt and pepper and squeeze over lemon juice to serve. SERVES 2.

Store-bought dips and salsas can serve as great fillings for sandwiches or rolls as well as instant sauces. Do a bit of your own research and you're bound to develop a list of favourites. Mine include hummus, tzatziki and baba ghanoush.

vegetable antipasti couscous

1 cup (180g) instant couscous
1¼ cups (310ml) boiling water
sea salt and cracked black pepper
30g butter, chopped
½ cup (50g) finely grated parmesan
250g mixed marinated antipasti vegetables, drained
¼ cup torn basil leaves
130g feta

Place couscous in a heatproof bowl and pour over boiling water. Cover tightly with plastic wrap and allow to stand for 5 minutes or until the water has been absorbed. Remove plastic wrap and stir in salt, pepper and butter. Toss through parmesan, vegetables, basil and feta. SERVES 2.

instant thai noodle salad

100g dried bean thread noodles
1 carrot, finely sliced
50g snow pea (mange tout) sprouts, trimmed
1 cucumber, sliced
½ cup coriander (cilantro) leaves
½ cup mint leaves
½ cup roasted unsalted peanuts or cashew nuts
150g firm tofu, sliced
¼ cup (60ml) sweet chilli sauce
¼ cup (60ml) lime juice
2 tablespoons fish sauce

Place noodles in a heatproof bowl and pour over boiling water to cover. Allow to stand for 5 minutes then drain and rinse under cold water. Toss the noodles with carrots, snow peas, cucumber, coriander, mint, nuts and tofu. Combine chilli sauce, lime juice and fish sauce, pour over salad and serve. SERVES 2.

INSTANT THAI NOODLE SALAD

smoked salmon bruschetta

125g cream cheese
1 tablespoon chopped dill leaves
2 tablespoons lemon juice
¼ cup coarsely chopped cornichons (G)
sea salt and cracked black pepper
4 slices rye bread, toasted
1 x 175g hot-smoked salmon fillet, cut into chunks (G)

Combine cream cheese, dill, lemon juice, cornichons, salt and pepper in a bowl and mix well. Spread cheese mixture on toast and top with salmon to serve. You could substitute slices of cold-smoked salmon if the hot-smoked variety isn't available. **SERVES 2.**

chicken, cashew & chilli salad

100g dried bean thread noodles
½ store-bought barbecued chicken, flesh shredded
1 cucumber, sliced
1 tomato, cut into wedges
⅓ cup (50g) roasted unsalted cashews
¼ cup coriander (cilantro) leaves
¼ cup basil leaves
chilli dressing
¼ cup (60ml) sweet chilli sauce
1½ teaspoons soy sauce

Place noodles in a heatproof bowl and pour over boiling water. Allow to stand for 5 minutes or until tender, drain. Toss noodles with chicken, cucumber, tomato, cashews, coriander and basil. To make the dressing, combine sweet chilli and soy and toss through the salad. **SERVES 2.**

shortcut steak sandwich

4 thick slices crusty bread
butter, for spreading
¼ cup (70g) onion relish, mustard or chutney
1 tomato, sliced
8 slices store-bought rare roast beef
8 slices cheddar
rocket (arugula) or salad leaves, to serve

Place the bread on a baking tray and place under a hot grill and toast one side only. Butter 2 of the untoasted sides and spread the remaining 2 untoasted sides with the relish. Top with tomato, beef and cheese. Place under the grill and cook for 2 minutes or until cheese is melted. Serve with rocket and buttered toast. **SERVES 2.**

ginger & soy-infused tofu

300g silken firm tofu, thickly sliced
1 tablespoon finely grated ginger
⅓ cup (80ml) soy sauce
2 tablespoons brown sugar
3 green onions (scallions), finely sliced
2 teaspoons sesame oil
2 tablepoons sesame seeds
2 carrots, shredded
100g snow peas (mange tout), finely sliced

Place tofu in a shallow dish. Combine the ginger, soy, sugar, green onion and sesame oil and pour over the tofu, allow to stand for 5 minutes then turn. Toss together sesame seeds, carrot and snow peas and place on serving plates. Top with the tofu and spoon the marinade over as a dressing. **SERVES 2.**

TORN TOMATO & MOZZARELLA SALAD WITH TAPENADE DRESSING

LENTIL, ARTICHOKE & GOAT'S CHEESE SALAD

torn tomato & mozzarella salad with tapenade dressing

2 ripe tomatoes
1 large buffalo mozzarella or 4 bocconcini
2 slices char-grilled or toasted sourdough bread
cracked black pepper
40g rocket (arugula) leaves
¼ cup basil leaves
tapenade dressing
1 tablespoon store-bought black olive tapenade (G)
2 tablespoons olive oil
1 teaspoon balsamic vinegar

Tear tomatoes and cheese into chunks. Place bread on serving plates and press the tomato lightly into the bread. Sprinkle with pepper and top with mozzarella, rocket and basil. To make the dressing, combine tapenade, oil and vinegar and spoon over the salad. SERVES 2.

Mozzarella can be made from pasteurised cow's milk, but the most prized variety is made from fresh buffalo milk. Bocconcini means "mouthful" in Italian and that's precisely what these bite-sized morsels of fresh mozzarella are.

lentil, artichoke & goat's cheese salad

400g can lentils, drained and rinsed
1 tablespoon red wine vinegar
1 teaspoon sugar
1 tablespoon olive oil
sea salt and cracked black pepper
1 cup flatleaf parsley leaves, torn
280g jar marinated artichoke hearts, drained and halved
½ store-bought barbecued chicken, thickly sliced
150g goat's cheese, to serve

Place lentils, vinegar, sugar, olive oil, salt and pepper in a glass or ceramic bowl and stand for 5 minutes. Toss the lentil mixture with parsley, artichokes and chicken. Serve with sliced goat's cheese. SERVES 2.

asian ginger prawn & noodle salad

150g dried rice stick noodles
12 cooked prawns (shrimp), peeled with tails intact
2 green onions (scallions), finely sliced
1 long red chilli, finely sliced
½ cup coriander (cilantro) leaves
50g snow peas (mange tout), shredded
2 tablespoons soy sauce
1 teaspoon grated ginger
1 teaspoon sugar

Place noodles in a heatproof bowl and cover with boiling water. Stand for 10 minutes or until tender, drain. Toss the noodles with the prawns, onion, chilli, coriander, snow peas, soy, ginger and sugar. SERVES 2.

ASIAN GINGER PRAWN & NOODLE SALAD

toasted italian bread salad

3 thick slices sourdough bread, toasted and torn
4 ripe tomatoes, torn
½ cup (75g) pitted Kalamata olives
425g can tuna, drained
1 cup flatleaf parsley leaves
white vinegar dressing
2 tablespoons white wine vinegar
2 tablespoons olive oil
1 small clove garlic, crushed
cracked black pepper

To make the white wine vinegar dressing, place vinegar, oil, garlic and pepper in a bowl and whisk to combine. Add bread and tomato to the dressing and toss lightly together. Add olives, tuna and parsley and toss to combine. **SERVES 2**.

smoked salmon & avocado enchiladas

4 small flour tortillas
⅓ cup (80g) sour cream
8 slices (200g) smoked salmon
½ avocado, sliced
100g watercress sprigs
⅓ cup flatleaf parsley leaves
½ cucumber, sliced
2 green onions (scallions), sliced
2 tablespoons lime juice
sea salt and cracked black pepper

Warm tortillas in a warm oven, microwave or toaster until heated through. Spread with the sour cream and top with salmon. Toss together the avocado, watercress, parsley, cucumber, onion, lime juice, salt and pepper. Spoon the salad mixture over the salmon. Roll tortillas to enclose the filling and serve. **SERVES 2**.

smoked chicken & lemon-mayo salad

250g cooked smoked chicken breast, sliced
1 baby cos lettuce, trimmed and leaves separated
1 small cucumber, sliced lengthways
¼ cup (40g) finely grated parmesan
lemon-mayo dressing
⅓ cup (100g) whole-egg mayonnaise
1 tablespoon lemon juice
1 tablespoon chopped basil leaves
sea salt

To make lemon-mayo dressing, place mayonnaise, lemon juice, basil and salt in a bowl and stir to combine. Arrange smoked chicken, lettuce, cucumber slices and parmesan on serving plates. Drizzle lemon-mayo dressing over the salad to serve. **SERVES 2.**

speedy chicken tabouli

¾ cup (120g) fine cracked wheat (burghul) (G)
1½ cups (375ml) boiling water
½ store-bought barbecued chicken, flesh chopped
2 tomatoes, chopped
2 green onions (scallions), chopped
½ cup chopped flatleaf parsley leaves
½ cup chopped mint leaves
2 tablespoons olive oil
1 tablespoon lemon juice
sea salt and cracked black pepper
store-bought hummus, to serve
flatbread and lemon, to serve

Place cracked wheat in a bowl. Add boiling water and cover with plastic wrap, set aside for 20 minutes or until the wheat is soft. Place chicken, tomato, onion, parsley, mint, oil, lemon juice, salt and pepper and wheat into a small bowl and toss to combine. Serve with hummus, flatbread and lemon. **SERVES 2.**

MOZZARELLA & WHITE BEAN BRUSCHETTA

AVOCADO, TUNA & TOMATO SALAD

mozzarella & white bean bruschetta

400g can white (cannellini) beans, drained
1 clove garlic, crushed
2 tablespoons olive oil
1 tablespoon lemon juice
¼ cup roughly chopped flatleaf parsley leaves
sea salt and cracked black pepper
4 slices sourdough bread, toasted
40g rocket (arugula) leaves
2 large buffalo mozzarella, torn in half
8 slices prosciutto
extra olive oil, for drizzling
lemon wedges, to serve

Place beans, garlic, oil and lemon juice into a bowl and mash roughly with a fork until mixture is a rough paste. Stir through parsley, salt and pepper. Spread mixture over toast and place on serving plates. Top with rocket, mozzarella and prosciutto. Drizzle with the extra oil and serve with lemon wedges. SERVES 2.

A well-stocked pantry is a busy cook's best insurance. Canned tuna is a great standby that can transform a meal in seconds flat. Canned beans, chickpeas and lentils also have a role in the time-poor kitchen arsenal.

avocado, tuna & tomato salad

1 avocado, cut into quarters
2 x 125g cans tuna slices, drained
2 tomatoes, thickly sliced
½ cup flatleaf parsley leaves
sea salt and cracked black pepper
olive oil, for drizzling
1 teaspoon ground sumac (G)
lemon wedges, to serve

Arrange avocado, tuna, tomato and parsley on serving plates. Sprinkle with salt and pepper and drizzle with oil. Sprinkle with sumac and serve with lemon wedges. SERVES 2.

shaved haloumi salad with lemon-honey dressing

150g haloumi (G)
2 tomatoes, thickly sliced
¼ cup mint leaves
1 cucumber, thickly sliced
2 stalks celery, thickly sliced
lemon-honey dressing
2 tablespoons lemon juice
1 tablespoon honey
1 tablespoon olive oil
cracked black pepper

Shave haloumi with a wide vegetable peeler. Combine with tomato, mint, cucumber and celery. Make lemon-honey dressing by combining lemon juice, honey, oil and pepper. Spoon over salad and serve. SERVES 2.

SHAVED HALOUMI SALAD WITH LEMON-HONEY DRESSING

preserved lemon, tuna & bean salad

400g can white (cannellini) beans, rinsed and drained
425g can tuna, drained
1 tablespoon shredded preserved lemon rind (G)
1 cup flatleaf parsley leaves
sea salt and cracked black pepper
lemon juice, to serve
toasted sourdough, to serve

Combine beans and tuna in a medium bowl, add preserved lemon, parsley, salt and pepper and mix together well. Pour lemon juice over the salad and serve with slices of toasted sourdough. SERVES 2.

minted pea & feta salad

2 cups (240g) frozen peas
½ cup mint leaves
1 tablespoon lemon juice
2 tablespoons olive oil
cracked black pepper
50g baby spinach or salad leaves
100g feta
6 slices prosciutto
lavosh bread, to serve

Place peas in a heatproof bowl and pour over boiling water. Allow to stand for 2 minutes or until peas are just tender. Drain and refresh under cold water. Combine peas, mint, lemon juice, oil and pepper and toss to combine. Divide the spinach between plates and top with pea mixture, feta and prosciutto. Serve with lavosh bread. SERVES 2.

cheat's chicken caesar salad

½ store-bought barbecued chicken, flesh sliced
2 baby cos lettuce, halved and trimmed
¼ cup (20g) shaved parmesan
100g store-bought pita crisps, crostini or croutons
4 slices prosciutto
cracked black pepper
Caesar dressing
½ cup (150g) whole-egg mayonnaise
1 tablespoon lemon juice
1 teaspoon Dijon mustard

Combine chicken, lettuce, parmesan, pita crisps and prosciutto and arrange on plates. To make the Caesar dressing, whisk together mayonnaise, lemon juice and mustard. Pour over the salad and sprinkle with pepper. **SERVES 2**.

chicken salad with coconut dressing

40g salad leaves
1 carrot, finely sliced
1 cucumber, finely sliced
½ store-bought barbecued chicken, flesh shredded
⅓ cup coriander (cilantro) leaves
⅓ cup basil leaves
½ cup (70g) dry-roasted peanuts, coarsely chopped
coconut dressing
1 long red chilli, chopped
⅓ cup (80ml) coconut cream
1 tablespoon lime juice
1 teaspoon brown sugar
1 teaspoon fish sauce

Arrange the salad leaves, carrot, cucumber, chicken, coriander and basil on serving plates. To make the dressing, combine chilli, coconut cream, lime juice, sugar and fish sauce. Pour the dressing over the salad, sprinkle with peanuts to serve. **SERVES 2**.

CHEATS 1.

breakfast & brunch

With everyone's life on fast forward, weekends are utterly precious for spending time with family and friends. Getting together over breakfast or brunch is a lovely relaxed way to catch up as everyone expects a casual meal. The food doesn't have to be complicated but we've tweaked some of the traditional favourites to inject a bit of surprise into the menu.

cinnamon apples
with brown sugar yoghurt

RIGHT: Core 2 apples and cut into thick slices. Place in a medium non-stick frying pan over medium heat with 1 cinnamon stick, 25g butter, 2 tablespoons water and 2 tablespoons maple syrup. Allow to simmer for 5 minutes each side or until soft. Place warm or cold apples on serving plates, serve with a generous spoonful of natural yoghurt. Sprinkle with brown sugar to serve. **SERVES 2.**

berry & maple crunch

BELOW: Toss together 1 cup (90g) rolled oats, ½ cup (80g) roughly chopped almonds and ¼ cup (75g) sunflower or pepita seeds with ½ cup (125ml) maple syrup. Place on a baking tray lined with non-stick baking paper and bake in a preheated 180°C (355°F) oven for 12–15 minutes or until golden and crisp. Place raspberries, strawberries or mixed berries into a glass. Top with a few spoonfuls of thick natural yoghurt and the crunchy oat mixture. **SERVES 6.**

We've come up with a fresh take on the classic combination of fruit and yoghurt to inject renewed appeal into the traditional breakfast starters. Berries and cereal complete this appealing array.

apple & strawberry bircher

ABOVE: Combine 1 cup (90g) rolled oats and ¾ cup (180ml) apple juice in a bowl. Allow to stand for 5 minutes. Add 1 grated green apple, a pinch ground cinnamon, ¼ cup (35g) toasted roughly chopped almonds, ½ cup (140g) thick natural yoghurt and 1 tablespoon maple syrup and mix gently. Spoon into serving bowls and top with sliced seasonal fruits such as strawberries, peach, pear or blueberries. Drizzle with a little extra maple syrup and serve. **SERVES 2.**

baked peaches
with rosewater yoghurt

LEFT: Halve 2 peaches and remove the stones. Place cut side up in a baking dish lined with non-stick baking paper, and sprinkle cut sides with sugar. Bake in a preheated 180°C (355°F) oven for 20 minutes or until soft and golden. Combine 1 cup (280g) thick vanilla yoghurt with ½ teaspoon rosewater. Place peaches on serving plates, top with rosewater yoghurt and chopped unsalted pistachio nuts. **SERVES 2.**

egg rolls

RIGHT: Heat a medium non-stick frying pan over high heat. For each egg roll whisk together 1 egg with sea salt and cracked black pepper. Pour egg into the hot pan and swirl to coat the entire surface of the pan. Cook for 1 minute or until egg is just set. Remove from pan and top with any filling of your choice such as smoked salmon, sour cream and watercress or roasted tomatoes, baby spinach leaves and crispy bacon. Roll to enclose and serve warm. **MAKES 1.**

asparagus bruschetta

BELOW: Soft-boil 2 eggs in boiling water for 4 minutes, remove and plunge into cold water before peeling. Brush 4 large slices bread with 1 tablespoon olive oil combined with 1 teaspoon finely grated lemon rind. Place bread on a preheated char-grill pan (broiler) and cook on both sides until toasted. Top the bruschetta with blanched asparagus spears, very thin slices of prosciutto, soft-boiled eggs, grated parmesan, sea salt and cracked black pepper. **SERVES 2.**

When the event calls for a more substantial start to the day it's hard to go past the egg in its many guises. Beans are also a versatile and very popular choice. Team with bacon, for a sure winner!

bacon & beans

ABOVE: Cook 4 rashers chopped bacon in a frying pan over medium–high heat until crisp. Add a 400g can drained and rinsed white (cannellini) or butter beans, 150g halved cherry tomatoes and 1 teaspoon thyme leaves. Cook for 4 minutes or until tomatoes are just soft and the beans are heated through. Sprinkle with sea salt and cracked black pepper and serve on hot buttered sourdough toast. **SERVES 2.**

pancetta baked eggs

LEFT: Line 6 greased ½-cup (125ml) capacity muffin tins with 2–3 slices of pancetta to cover the base and sides. Whisk together 3 eggs, ½ cup (125ml) cream, 1 tablespoon torn basil leaves, ¼ cup (20g) grated parmesan, sea salt and cracked black pepper. Pour mixture into the pancetta-lined tins and bake in a preheated 180°C (355°F) oven for 12 minutes or until the eggs are just set. Serve with hot buttered toast. **SERVES 6.**

roasted tomato tarts

RIGHT: Cut 1 sheet (25 cm x 25cm) of thawed store-bought puff pastry into 4 and place on baking trays lined with non-stick baking paper. Combine 1 cup (200g) fresh ricotta with ¼ cup (20g) grated parmesan, sea salt and cracked black pepper. Spread the ricotta over the pastries leaving a border. Top each pastry with 3 cherry tomatoes. Drizzle with olive oil and sprinkle with thyme leaves. Bake in a preheated 180°C (355°F) oven for 25–30 minutes or until pastry is puffed and golden. **MAKES 4.**

simple banana bread

BELOW: Combine 1⅔ cups (220g) plain (all-purpose) flour, 1½ teaspoons baking powder, ⅓ cup (75g) caster (superfine) sugar, ⅓ cup (110g) brown sugar, 1 teaspoon ground cinnamon and 1 teaspoon vanilla extract. Make a well in the centre, add 2 eggs, ½ cup (125ml) vegetable oil and 3 mashed bananas (1½ cups) and mix to combine. Pour into a greased 20cm x 10cm x 10cm loaf tin. Sprinkle with brown sugar and bake in a preheated 160°C (320°F) oven for 60 minutes or until cooked when tested.

Whether you're looking for inspiration for brunch or some great travelling fare to take on a picnic or road trip, these options strike just the right balance between light and filling and classic and original.

berry french toast

ABOVE: Spread 2 thick slices of brioche with a mixture of ⅓ cup (60g) cream cheese mixed with 2 tablespoons caster (superfine) sugar and ¼ teaspoon finely grated lime rind. Top with slightly thawed frozen raspberries or blueberries and sandwich together with extra slices of brioche. Heat a little butter in a pan and cook the sandwiches for 3 minutes each side or until golden brown. Serve warm for breakfast, brunch or with ice-cream for dessert. **SERVES 2.**

mini bacon & egg rolls

LEFT: Cut the tops from 8 small dinner rolls and scoop out the soft bread inside. Whisk together 4 eggs, 1 cup (250ml) cream, 2 tablespoons chopped chives, sea salt flakes and cracked black pepper. Remove the rind from 8 bacon rashers. Place the rolls on a baking tray and line the cavities with the bacon. Pour in the egg mixture and bake in a preheated 160°C (320°F) oven for 25–30 minutes or until the egg is just set. Serve the rolls warm or cold. **MAKES 8.**

FAST FLAVOUR

The secret to fabulous fast food is not the number of ingredients you use or the complexity of their preparation. Rather, it's the freshest produce, simple combinations and the way you cook them. Fire up the barbie or grill pan for fantastic results in a matter of minutes. Those char-grill lines are not just for looks — they're also the key to wonderful, intense flavours.

T-BONE STEAK WITH PORCINI SALT

SALMON WITH PRESERVED LEMON MAYO

t-bone steak with porcini salt

10g dried porcini mushrooms (G)
1 tablespoon sea salt flakes
2 x 300g t-bone steaks
olive oil, for brushing
½ teaspoon cracked black pepper
hand-cut chips and salad, to serve

Place porcini and salt into a small food processor, blender or mortar and pestle and grind until very fine. Brush the steaks with a little olive oil and sprinkle both sides with a little porcini salt and pepper. Preheat a char-grill pan (broiler) or barbecue to medium and cook steaks for 4–5 minutes each side or until cooked to your liking. Sprinkle with extra porcini salt and serve with hand-cut chips and a green salad. SERVES 2.

Who would have thought that the simple combination of dry porcini and salt would be such a flavour sensation? It is one of my real favourites in the book and already has the nickname of 'magic porcini dust'. Sprinkle on chips, grilled or roasted chicken, lamb or beef and expect to be awestruck.

salmon with preserved lemon mayo

2 x 200g salmon fillets
10 asparagus spears, trimmed
olive oil, for brushing
sea salt and cracked black pepper
1 baby cos lettuce, trimmed
preserved lemon mayo
½ cup (150g) store-bought whole-egg mayonnaise
2 tablespoons finely chopped preserved lemon (G)
1 tablespoon finely chopped chervil leaves

To make preserved lemon mayo, place mayonnaise, preserved lemon and chervil in a bowl, stir to combine. Cut salmon fillets lengthways into three slices. Brush salmon and asparagus with oil, sprinkle with salt and pepper. Preheat a char-grill pan (broiler) or barbecue to medium-high and cook salmon and asparagus for 1–2 minutes each side, or until salmon is cooked to your liking and asparagus is crisp but tender. Divide lettuce between serving plates, top with salmon and asparagus and serve with preserved lemon mayo. SERVES 2.

peppered pork with apple slaw

4 x 75g pork loin steaks
olive oil, for brushing
2 teaspoons cracked black pepper
pinch dried chilli flakes
1 teaspoon sea salt flakes
apple slaw
1 green apple, coarsely grated
1 cup shredded white cabbage
2 tablespoons chopped chives
¼ cup (75g) whole-egg mayonnaise
1 teaspoon honey

Brush pork lightly with olive oil. Combine pepper, chilli and salt and sprinkle over both sides of the pork loin. Preheat a char-grill pan (broiler) or barbecue to high, cook for 2–3 minutes each side or until cooked to your liking, set aside to rest. To make the apple slaw, combine the apple, cabbage and chives. Mix mayonnaise and honey together, pour over the slaw and toss to coat. Place pork on plates and serve with the apple slaw. SERVES 2.

PEPPERED PORK WITH APPLE SLAW

garlic-grilled chicken with rocket salsa

4 x 140g chicken thigh fillets
2 tablespoons olive oil
6 cloves garlic, crushed
1 tablespoon oregano leaves
sea salt and cracked black pepper
shredded rocket salsa
40g rocket (arugula) leaves, shredded
¼ cup (40g) pitted and halved olives
40g shaved parmesan
1 tablespoon balsamic vinegar
1 tablespoon olive oil

Place chicken thigh, oil, garlic, oregano, salt and pepper in a shallow dish and toss to combine. Allow chicken to marinate for 10 minutes. To make the salsa, combine rocket, olives, parmesan, vinegar and oil and toss gently to combine. Preheat a char-grill pan (broiler) or barbecue to hot and cook the chicken, basting frequently with the marinade, for 4–5 minutes each side or until cooked through. Place chicken on serving plates and serve with the rocket salsa. **SERVES 2**.

prawns with lemongrass & lime butter

12 large green (raw) prawns (shrimp), unpeeled
2 stalks lemongrass
1 teaspoon finely grated lime rind
60g butter, softened
sea salt
iceberg lettuce wedges, to serve

To prepare prawns remove heads and cut down the underside of the shell to halfway through and press to flatten. Combine lemongrass, lime rind, butter and salt in a mortar and pestle and pound until well combined. Melt butter mixture in microwave or small saucepan over low heat, brush prawns with the mixture. Preheat a char-grill pan (broiler) or barbecue to medium-high and cook prawns for 3 minutes or until cooked through. Serve with lettuce wedges. **SERVES 2**.

harissa chicken & sweet potato

1 tablespoon harissa (G)
2 tablespoons olive oil
¼ cup roughly chopped coriander (cilantro) leaves
sea salt
4 x 140g chicken thigh fillets, halved
500g orange sweet potato (kumara), peeled and thinly sliced
40g baby spinach leaves
store-bought tzatziki, to serve

Combine harissa, oil, coriander leaves and salt in a bowl. Add chicken and sweet potato and toss to coat. Preheat a char-grill pan (broiler) or barbecue to medium and cook chicken and sweet potato for 4–5 minutes each side or until browned and cooked through. Divide spinach between plates, top with chicken and sweet potato and serve with tzatziki. **SERVES 2**.

chicken, lime & coriander quesadillas

75g cream cheese, softened
2 tablespoons lime juice
1 long green chilli, seeded and chopped
3 green onions (scallions), finely sliced
2 cups coarsely chopped cooked chicken breast
sea salt and cracked black pepper
½ cup coriander (cilantro) leaves
1 cup (120g) grated cheddar
8 small corn or flour tortillas
vegetable oil, for brushing
lime wedges and tomato, coriander and onion salad, to serve

Place cream cheese, lime juice and chilli in a bowl and mix well. Stir through onion, chicken, salt and pepper. Spread the chicken mixture over half the tortillas. Top with coriander, cheese and remaining tortillas and brush both sides with a little oil. Preheat a char-grill pan (broiler) or barbecue to medium and cook the filled quesadillas for 2 minutes each side or until warmed through and crisp on the outside. Serve with lime wedges and tomato, coriander and onion salad. **SERVES 2**.

CURRY-CRUSTED CHICKEN & COCONUT NOODLES

HARISSA-SPICED BARBECUED LAMB

curry-crusted chicken & coconut noodles

2 x 200g chicken breast fillets, halved lengthways
2 teaspoons Thai green curry paste
2 tablespoons oil
lime wedges, to serve
coconut and coriander noodles
100g dried rice stick noodles
1 teaspoon sugar
1 tablespoon lime juice
4 green onions (scallions), sliced
¾ cup coriander (cilantro) leaves
1 long green chilli, sliced
100ml coconut milk
1 tablespoon fish sauce

To make the coconut and coriander noodles, place noodles in a heatproof bowl and cover with boiling water. Stand for 10 minutes or until tender, drain and rinse until cool. Dissolve sugar in lime juice, pour over noodles and toss with onion, coriander, chilli, coconut milk and fish sauce until combined. Divide noodles between serving plates. Brush the chicken on both sides with the combined curry paste and oil to lightly coat. Preheat a char-grill pan (broiler) or barbecue to high, cook chicken for 2-3 minutes each side or until cooked through. Place on top of the noodles and serve with lime wedges. **SERVES 2.**

You might be surprised at the many uses we've found for the condiments we keep in the test kitchen fridges. Red and green Thai curry pastes, Indian tandoor and curry blends and chilli jam provide fast and spicy flavour hits when used as bastes or marinades for grilled or roasted meats, seafood and vegetables.

harissa-spiced barbecued lamb

1 x 200g lamb backstrap (boneless loin), trimmed
2 teaspoons harissa or chilli paste (G)
1 tablespoon olive oil
2 tablespoons lemon juice
2 teaspoons chopped oregano leaves
sea salt and cracked black pepper
40g baby spinach leaves
2 tomatoes, sliced
¼ cup mint leaves
olive oil, for drizzling
2 flatbreads
100g store-bought baba ghanoush
lemon wedges, to serve

Place lamb in a shallow container. Combine harissa, oil, lemon juice, oregano, salt and pepper and pour over the lamb. Allow to marinate for 15 minutes. Preheat char-grill pan (broiler) or barbecue to medium-high, cook lamb for 4 minutes each side or until done to your liking. To serve, place spinach on serving plates and top with tomato, mint and a drizzle of olive oil. Slice lamb and divide between serving plates with flatbread, baba ghanoush and lemon wedges. **SERVES 2.**

prosciutto-wrapped steaks with blue cheese

2 x 220g thick sirloin or eye fillet steaks, trimmed
2 field mushrooms, stalks trimmed
1 tablespoon olive oil
1 tablespoon balsamic vinegar
cracked black pepper
1 tablespoon mustard
4 slices prosciutto
50g baby spinach leaves
70g soft blue cheese

Brush steaks and mushrooms with the combined oil and balsamic and sprinkle generously with pepper. Spread steaks with mustard, wrap in prosciutto. Preheat a char-grill pan (broiler) or barbecue to medium-high. Cook steaks and mushrooms for 5 minutes each side or until done to your liking. Divide spinach between serving plates and top with mushroom and steak. Finish with a wedge of cheese and allow cheese to melt slightly before serving. **SERVES 2.**

PROSCIUTTO-WRAPPED STEAKS WITH BLUE CHEESE

grilled miso-ginger chicken

2 tablespoons miso paste (G)
2 tablespoons soy sauce
2 teaspoons grated ginger
2 teaspoons sesame oil
2 x 200g chicken breast fillets, cut lengthways in thirds
ginger-snow pea salad
150g snow peas (mange tout), finely sliced
1½ tablespoons pickled ginger (gari) (G)
1 tablespoon sesame seeds, toasted

To make salad, place snow peas in a bowl, cover with boiling water for 1 minute, drain. Place snow peas, ginger and sesame seeds in a small bowl and toss to combine. Cover and set aside. Combine miso, soy, ginger and sesame oil in a separate bowl, add chicken and marinate for 5 minutes. Preheat a char-grill pan (broiler) or barbecue to medium-high and cook chicken 2 minutes each side, or until chicken is cooked through. Divide salad and chicken between serving plates. **SERVES 2.**

spice-grilled steak with chilli salsa

2 teaspoons smoked paprika
½ teaspoon cracked black pepper
2 teaspoons finely chopped thyme leaves
sea salt
2 x 220g thick sirloin or rib eye steaks
olive oil, for brushing
chilli salsa
3 long red chillies, halved lengthways, seeds removed
1 avocado, thickly sliced
1½ tablespoons lime juice
¼ cup coriander (cilantro) leaves

Combine paprika, pepper, thyme and salt. Brush steaks with a little oil and sprinkle both sides with the spice mix. Preheat a char-grill pan (broiler) or barbecue to medium-high and cook steaks and chillies, skin side down, for 3 minutes each side or until the steaks are cooked to your liking and the chilli is slightly charred. Place the steaks on serving plates. To make the chilli salsa combine chilli with avocado, lime juice, coriander and salt. To serve, pile salsa on top of steaks. **SERVES 2.**

chicken with sumac & almond couscous

1 tablespoon olive oil
2 cloves garlic, crushed
2 x 200g chicken breast fillets, halved lengthways
sea salt and sumac, for sprinkling
baby English spinach leaves, to serve
almond couscous
1 cup (200g) instant couscous
1 cup (250ml) boiling water
pinch chilli flakes
25g butter
3 green onions (scallions), finely sliced
⅓ cup (45g) toasted slivered almonds

To make almond couscous, combine couscous and water in a small heatproof bowl, cover with plastic wrap and set aside for 5 minutes. Remove plastic wrap, fluff couscous with a fork and stir in chilli, butter, onion and almonds. Combine oil and garlic, brush over chicken and sprinkle with salt and sumac. Preheat a char-grill pan (broiler) or barbecue to medium–high and cook chicken for 3 minutes each side, or until cooked through. Divide the couscous between plates, top with chicken and serve with spinach. **SERVES 2**.

sage veal cutlets with baby leeks

4 x 125g veal cutlets
4 sprigs sage
4 baby leeks, trimmed and halved
olive oil, for brushing
sea salt and cracked black pepper
salad leaves, to serve
buttermilk dressing
½ cup (125ml) buttermilk
½ cup finely chopped flatleaf parsley leaves
1 teaspoon finely grated lemon rind

To make buttermilk dressing, combine buttermilk, parsley and lemon rind in a bowl and mix well. Set aside. Place a sage sprig on each cutlet and tie with kitchen string. Brush leeks and veal with olive oil, sprinkle with salt and pepper. Preheat a char-grill pan (broiler) or barbecue to medium–high and cook veal and leeks for 4 minutes each side or until veal is cooked to your liking and leeks are soft and golden. Place salad leaves and leeks on serving plates, top with cutlets and drizzle with dressing. **SERVES 2**.

EGGPLANT SALAD WITH YOGHURT DRESSING

BARBECUED SPINACH & MOZZARELLA PIZZA

eggplant salad with yoghurt dressing

2 eggplant (aubergines) (600g), sliced
⅓ cup (80ml) olive oil
1½ teaspoons ground cumin
1½ teaspoons smoked paprika
sea salt and cracked black pepper
200g haloumi, sliced
400g can chickpeas (garbanzos), drained and rinsed
1 punnet (250g) cherry tomatoes, halved
¼ cup flatleaf parsley leaves, roughly chopped
1 teaspoon sumac (G)
minted yoghurt dressing
⅓ cup mint leaves, finely chopped
¾ cup (210g) thick natural yoghurt
1 clove garlic, crushed
2 teaspoons lemon juice

To make the dressing, combine mint, yoghurt, garlic, lemon juice and salt. Brush both sides of the eggplant with combined olive oil, cumin, paprika, salt and pepper. Preheat a char-grill pan (broiler) or barbecue to medium. Cook eggplant, in batches, for 2 minutes each side or until golden. Cook haloumi 1 minute each side or until lightly browned. Toss together chickpeas, tomatoes and parsley in a small bowl. Divide the dressing between serving plates. Top with layers of eggplant, haloumi, and chickpea salad. Sprinkle with sumac to serve. SERVES 2.

It's the finishing touches that turn an everyday meal into an overnight sensation. A generous sprinkling of tangy sumac gives a zesty lift to the eggplant salad as well as an intriguing dusting of purple. Speedy pickled onions elevate a mundane grill into something more memorable.

barbecued spinach & mozzarella pizza

200g English spinach leaves
2 rounds pita bread
240g fresh ricotta
2 teaspoons finely grated lemon rind
2 teaspoons lemon thyme leaves
6 bocconcini, halved
8 slices pancetta
rocket (arugula) leaves, to serve

Place spinach in a medium bowl and cover with boiling water for 2 minutes, drain. Squeeze out any remaining moisture using absorbent paper, then roughly chop. Spread pita bread with ricotta and top with spinach, lemon rind, thyme, bocconcini and pancetta. Preheat a char-grill pan (broiler) or barbecue to medium and place the pizza on the cooking surface. Close the lid of the barbecue or place a lid over the pan and cook for 5 minutes or until the base is golden and the cheese is melted. Serve with rocket. SERVES 2.

herb-grilled steak with pickled onions

1 tablespoon thyme leaves
1 tablespoon oregano leaves
½ teaspoon cracked black pepper
sea salt
1 tablespoon olive oil
400g rump steak, trimmed
rocket (arugula) leaves, to serve
pickled onions
2 onions, cut into thick slices
olive oil, for brushing
¼ cup (60ml) malt vinegar
¼ cup (55g) brown sugar

To make the pickled onions, brush onions with oil and cook for 3–4 minutes each side or until well browned and soft. Combine vinegar and sugar in a shallow bowl. Add the hot onions and turn to coat. Cover and keep warm. Combine thyme, oregano, pepper, salt and oil, rub over both sides of steak and stand for 10 minutes. Preheat a char-grill pan (broiler) or barbecue to medium. Cook the steak for 4 minutes each side, or until cooked to your liking. Serve in thick slices with the onions and rocket. SERVES 2.

HERB-GRILLED STEAK WITH PICKLED ONIONS

grilled haloumi & fennel salad

¼ cup (60ml) olive oil
1 tablespoon cracked black pepper
500g fennel, sliced
250g haloumi, sliced
1 brown pear, finely sliced
30g rocket (arugula) leaves
walnut and chive dressing
1 tablespoon olive oil
1 tablespoon lemon juice
1 teaspoon Dijon mustard
½ cup (25g) walnuts
1 tablespoon finely chopped chives

To make dressing, place oil, lemon juice, mustard, walnuts and chives in a bowl and stir to combine. Place oil and pepper in a large bowl, add fennel and haloumi and turn to coat. Preheat a char-grill pan (broiler) or barbecue to medium–high, add fennel and cook for 2–3 minutes each side, or until tender and browned. Add haloumi and cook for 1–2 minutes each side or until cheese is warmed through and browned on the outside. Layer fennel with haloumi, pear and rocket and drizzle with dressing. **SERVES 2**.

chorizo salad with paprika dressing

3 x 150g chorizo sausages, cut thickly lengthways
1 red capsicum (bell pepper), quartered
160g chat (baby) potatoes, cooked and sliced
80g baby spinach leaves
paprika dressing
1 teaspoon smoked paprika
2 tablespons olive oil
1 tablespoon sherry or red wine vinegar
sea salt and cracked black pepper

To make paprika dressing, combine paprika, oil, vinegar, salt and pepper and whisk together. Preheat a char-grill pan (broiler) or barbecue to medium–high. Add chorizo to the pan and cook for 2–3 minutes each side or until crisp, set aside. Add capsicum to the pan and cook for 2–3 minutes each side or until lightly charred. To serve, place potato, spinach, chorizo and capsicum on plates and pour dressing over. **SERVES 2**.

italian salad with basil dressing

2 slices bread
2 zucchini (courgette), thickly sliced
2 Roma tomatoes, halved
⅓ cup (80ml) olive oil, for brushing
sea salt and cracked black pepper
1 clove garlic, halved
40g rocket (arugula) leaves
⅓ cup (55g) pitted Kalamata olives
basil dressing
¼ cup basil leaves, torn
¼ cup toasted pine nuts
2 tablespoons olive oil
2 tablespoons balsamic vinegar

Brush bread, zucchini and tomatoes with oil and sprinkle with salt and pepper. Preheat a char-grill pan (broiler) or barbecue to medium-high. Cook bread, zucchini and tomatoes on both sides until the bread is toasted and the vegetables are soft. Rub bread with the cut garlic. Place rocket on plates, top with bread, zucchini, tomatoes and olives. To make basil dressing, combine basil, pine nuts, oil and vinegar and spoon over salad. **SERVES 2.**

rosemary lamb burgers

400g lamb mince
1 teaspoon chopped rosemary leaves
2 tablespoons Dijon mustard
1 tablespoon honey
½ cup (35g) fresh breadcrumbs
1 egg yolk
sea salt and cracked black pepper
olive oil, for brushing
2 pieces Turkish bread, halved
¼ cup (70g) thick natural yoghurt
1 Lebanese cucumber, sliced
1 tablespoon torn mint leaves
40g rocket (arugula) leaves

Place lamb, rosemary, mustard, honey, breadcrumbs, egg yolk, salt and pepper in a bowl and mix to combine. Shape into 2 large flat patties and brush with oil. Preheat a char-grill pan (broiler) or barbecue to medium and cook patties for 5–8 minutes each side or until cooked to your liking. Place bread on the barbecue and toast. Spread 2 slices with yoghurt and top with cucumber, mint, lamb patties, rocket and remaining toast. **SERVES 2.**

GRILLED TOFU WITH CHILLI DRESSING

SKEWERED GARLIC & PARSLEY PRAWNS

grilled tofu with chilli dressing

100g dried rice stick noodles
300g firm tofu
12 asparagus spears
1 tablespoon sesame oil
1 tablespoon peanut oil
chilli dressing
1 long red chilli, chopped
¼ cup (60ml) soy sauce
1 tablespoon brown sugar
2 teaspoons finely grated ginger
2 tablespoons chopped roasted peanuts

To make the chilli dressing, combine chilli, soy, sugar, ginger and peanuts in a small bowl and set aside. Place noodles in another bowl, cover with boiling water for 10 minutes or until separated and tender, drain. Brush tofu and asparagus with the combined sesame and peanut oils. Preheat a char-grill pan (broiler) or barbecue to medium-high. Cook the tofu and asparagus for 3 minutes each side or until tofu is golden and asparagus is tender. To serve, divide the noodles between plates, top with grilled tofu and asparagus and spoon over the chilli dressing. SERVES 2.

Tofu (bean curd) is a wonderful ingredient because it readily absorbs whatever flavour you want to put with it. It also takes up the wonderful caramelised nuances from the char-grill. Be sure to buy the firmest grade of tofu for this dish as anything labelled silken or soft tofu will break up during cooking.

skewered garlic & parsley prawns

12–16 green (raw) prawns (shrimp), peeled with tails intact
12 small cloves garlic, unpeeled
2 tablespoons olive oil
1 tablespoon finely chopped flatleaf parsley leaves
sea salt and cracked black pepper
lemon wedges, to serve

Thread prawns and garlic onto skewers. Combine oil, parsley, salt and pepper and brush over the prawns. Preheat a char-grill pan (broiler) or barbecue to medium–high and cook prawns for 2–3 minutes each side or until they are pink and cooked through. Serve prawn skewers with lemon wedges. SERVES 2.

herbed veal steak sandwiches

2 x 200g veal schnitzels
1 tablespoon Dijon mustard
1 tablespoon finely chopped flatleaf parsley leaves
1 tablespoon finely chopped mint leaves
1 tablespoon finely chopped chives
4 slices bread
olive oil, for brushing
sea salt and cracked black pepper
2 tablespoons whole-egg mayonnaise
salad greens, to serve

Spread one side of veal with mustard. Combine the parsley, mint and chives and sprinkle half the herbs over the mustard. Fold the veal in half. Brush the veal and bread with olive oil, sprinkle with salt and pepper. Preheat a char-grill pan (broiler) or barbecue to hot, cook bread and veal for 2 minutes each side or until bread is charred and veal cooked through. Spread 2 slices of bread with mayonnaise and sprinkle with remaining herbs. Top the bread with veal and remaining bread and serve with salad greens. SERVES 2.

HERBED VEAL STEAK SANDWICHES

CHEATS 2.

marinades & rubs

*How often do you wish that you had access
to some magic potion that would transform
your mundane meals into memorable feasts?
As a matter of fact you probably do, or at least
the makings for any number of wonderful mixes
that will enhance meat, fish and vegetables.
Best of all, you need look no further than your
pantry or herb garden to find these ingredients.*

crushed juniper & sage marinade

RIGHT: Crush 1 tablespoon of juniper berries with the back of a spoon. Place juniper in a bowl with 6 sprigs of sage, ½ teaspoon sea salt flakes, ½ teaspoon cracked black pepper and a splash of olive oil. Use as marinade for chicken, duck, lamb or pork. Alternatively, spoon the marinade over the meat before roasting so the flavours permeate during the cooking process.

fennel & oregano rub

BELOW: Place 2 tablespoons of fennel seeds into a dry frying pan over medium heat and cook for 2–3 minutes or until fragrant. Place into a spice grinder with 1 tablespoon sea salt flakes and 2 tablespoons oregano leaves and grind until finely chopped. Use as a rub before roasting pork loin or leg or rub into pork fillet, steaks or cutlets. It's also great on lamb leg, cutlets or steaks.

It's not the number of different spices that makes a great blend, but the right balance of a few key flavours. Some, such as fennel and oregano, are ancient allies. Others are more recent happy unions.

eastern spice rub

ABOVE: Combine 1 tablespoon finely chopped oregano, 1 tablespoon finely chopped thyme leaves, 1 tablespoon sesame seeds, 1 tablespoon sumac and 1 teaspoon sea salt flakes in a small bowl. Sprinkle the rub over chicken, lamb, seafood or vegetables before you cook by barbecuing, roasting or pan-frying.

mixed pepper rub

LEFT: Combine 2 teaspoons sea salt flakes, 1 teaspoon white peppercorns, and 1 teaspoon black peppercorns, in a mortar and pestle and grind coarsely. Add 1 tablespoon of drained green peppercorns and crush lightly. Use as a rub for roasted and grilled beef, lamb, chicken and pork.

hoisin marinade

RIGHT: Combine ⅓ cup (80ml) hoisin sauce with 1 tablespoon finely grated ginger, ½ teaspoon Chinese five-spice powder and 1 teaspoon sesame oil in a small bowl. Spread or brush the marinade over chicken pieces, white fish fillets or pork fillet or cutlets before roasting, pan-frying or grilling. Or use as a baste during the cooking process.

thai lime & lemongrass marinade

BELOW: Place 3 stalks trimmed and chopped lemongrass, 2 teaspoons finely grated lime rind, ¼ cup (60ml) lime juice, 1 tablespoon fish sauce, 2 long red chillies, 1 tablespoon brown sugar, 1 tablespoon vegetable oil and 1 tablespoon grated ginger into a food processor and process in bursts until the mixture is finely chopped. Spread over chicken, fish or beef.

Short on time doesn't have to mean short on flavour. The best way to be sure your marinade flavours the base meat, chicken or fish is to coat it with a thick layer of the mix before roasting or grilling.

chilli jam marinade

ABOVE: Place 8 chopped long red chillies, 1 peeled onion, 2 cloves peeled garlic, ¼ cup (60ml) fish sauce and ¼ cup (55g) brown sugar in a food processor and process until very finely chopped. Place mixture into a non-stick frying pan and cook over medium–high heat until thick and browned. To use, spread over chicken, pork or beef and marinate for approximately 10 minutes before frying or barbecuing.

barbecue marinade

LEFT: Place 2 tablespoons Worcestershire sauce, 2 crushed cloves garlic, ½ cup (125ml) beer, 2 tablespoons tomato paste, 1 tablespoon brown sugar, sea salt and cracked black pepper in a small bowl and stir to combine. Use as a marinade for beef steak, lamb or chicken or brush on generously as a baste throughout the cooking process.

garlic & rosemary marinade

RIGHT: Combine 4 sliced cloves garlic, 3 rosemary sprigs cut into 3cm lengths, ¼ cup (60ml) olive oil, 1 tablespoon balsamic vinegar, 1 teaspoon sea salt and cracked black pepper in a small bowl. Use as a marinade for lamb, pork and chicken before grilling, pan-frying or roasting. Or use as a baste during the cooking process.

smoky barbecue rub

BELOW: Combine 1 tablespoon smoked paprika with 1 tablespoon chopped thyme leaves, 1 tablespoon chopped oregano leaves, ½ teaspoon cracked black pepper and 1 teaspoon sea salt flakes. Brush ribs, beef, pork, lamb, vegetables, chicken pieces or fillets with oil and sprinkle rub generously over before barbecuing, pan-frying or grilling.

A sure-fire way to spice things up is with a pungent mixture of herbs and spices. Garlic, pepper, salt, chilli and lemon all have a role in the savvy cook's arsenal of instant flavour boosters.

chinese salt & pepper spice mix

ABOVE: Place a small frying pan over medium-high heat. Add 1 teaspoon Sichuan peppercorns (G), 2 dry red chillies, 1 cinnamon stick, 1 teaspoon black peppercorns and 2 tablespoons sea salt. Cook, stirring, for 4 minutes or until the spices are fragrant. Place mixture into a small food processor or spice grinder and process until a rough powder forms. Sprinkle over seafood, poultry or pork before or after cooking.

preserved lemon & thyme paste

LEFT: Place ⅓ cup (70g) chopped preserved lemon (G), 2 tablespoon thyme leaves, 4 cloves garlic, sea salt flakes and cracked black pepper and ⅓ cup (80ml) olive oil into a food processor and process to a paste. Use the paste to marinate fish, chicken or vegetables. Alternatively, spoon the paste over meat before roasting so the flavours permeate during the cooking process.

ONE PAN

No longer solely the domain of campers and college students, we've taken a fresh approach to one-pan cooking and come up with some bold flavour and texture combinations that preserve all the simplicity of cooking in one vessel, but none of the blandness of the old-style recipes. Best of all, at meal's end you're left with one pan, not a sinkful of washing up.

MUSTARD LAMB WITH ROSEMARY POTATOES

CRISPY FISH WITH AVOCADO-LEMON SALSA

mustard lamb with rosemary potatoes

30g butter
600g chat (baby) potatoes, thickly sliced
½ cup (125ml) beef stock
1 tablespoon rosemary leaves
¾ cup (90g) frozen peas
350g lamb backstraps (boneless lamb loins)
2 tablespoons seed mustard
1 tablespoon brown sugar

Heat butter in a medium non-stick frying pan over medium heat. Add potatoes, stock and rosemary. Cover and cook for 10 minutes. Add peas and cook for a further 3 minutes or until potatoes are tender. Remove from pan and keep warm. Wipe out the pan and place over medium–high heat. Spread lamb with combined mustard and sugar. Cook for 4 minutes each side or until cooked to your liking. Slice the lamb and serve with the potatoes and peas. SERVES 2.

You could substitute lamb chops or cutlets for the backstraps in this recipe. Adding sugar to the mustard glaze, or to the balsamic in the case of the beetroot and fennel salad, promotes an almost instant, wonderful caramelising effect that intensifies the flavours and produces a rich, glossy finish on the meat or vegetables.

crispy fish with avocado-lemon salsa

2 x 200g thick firm white fish fillets
sea salt and cracked black pepper
olive oil, for pan-frying
30g butter
1½ tablespoons salted capers, rinsed
avocado-lemon salsa
1 small avocado, chopped
1 lemon, peeled and chopped
1 teaspoon sugar
1 long red chilli, seeded and sliced
¼ cup coriander (cilantro) leaves
30g rocket (arugula) leaves

To make the avocado and lemon salsa, place avocado, lemon, sugar, chilli, coriander, rocket, salt and pepper in a small bowl and gently combine. To cook the fish, heat a frying pan over high heat. Sprinkle fish with salt and pepper. Add oil and fish to the pan and cook for 4 minutes each side or until cooked through. The outside should be crisp and the middle just cooked through. Place fish on serving plates. Wipe out the pan and add butter and capers and cook for 2 minutes or until the capers are crispy. Spoon salsa onto fish, drizzle with brown butter and sprinkle with capers. SERVES 2.

caramelised beetroot & fennel salad

450g can baby beetroot, drained and halved
⅓ cup (80ml) balsamic vinegar
¼ cup (55g) brown sugar
2 fennel (260g), thinly sliced
½ cup flatleaf parsley leaves
150g goat's cheese

Place beetroot on absorbent paper to dry. Heat a non-stick frying pan over high heat. Add balsamic and sugar and cook for 3 minutes or until slightly thickened. Add beetroot and cook for 1 minute or until heated through and coated. Divide fennel, parsley and cheese between serving plates and top with the caramelised beetroot. SERVES 2.

CARAMELISED BEETROOT & FENNEL SALAD

lamb cutlets with pine nut crust

¾ cup (120g) pine nuts
sea salt and cracked black pepper
6 x 60g trimmed lamb cutlets
1 tablespoon olive oil
30g butter
150g English spinach leaves
1 tablespoon chopped dill

Place pine nuts, salt and pepper into a mortar and pestle and crush until pine nuts resemble breadcrumbs. Press cutlets into the pine nut mixture. Heat the oil in a non-stick frying pan over medium heat. Add the cutlets and cook for 2 minutes each side or until cooked to your liking. Place on a warm plate, cover and set aside. Melt butter in the pan, add spinach and dill and cook until wilted. Divide spinach between serving plates and top with the lamb cutlets. **SERVES 2**.

mushroom tarte tatin

50g butter
1 leek, trimmed and chopped
4 field mushrooms, thickly sliced
3 sprigs thyme
sea salt and cracked black pepper
2 sheets (25cm x 25cm) store-bought puff pastry, thawed
beaten egg, for brushing

Preheat oven to 180°C (355°F). Melt butter in a 23cm non-stick frying pan with an ovenproof handle, add leek and cook 1 minute. Remove leek from pan, add mushrooms and cook, in batches, for 2 minutes each side. Return leek and mushrooms to pan and add thyme. Cut 2 x 22cm-diameter rounds of pastry from the sheets and layer both pastry rounds on top of the mushroom mixture. Brush pastry top with beaten egg, place pan in preheated oven and bake for 15–20 minutes or until pastry is puffed and golden. Place a plate or wire rack on top of the pan and turn the tarte out to serve. **SERVES 2**.

fast polenta with mushrooms & goat's cheese

3 cups (750ml) boiling water
¾ cup (125g) instant polenta
75g butter
⅓ cup (25g) finely grated parmesan
1 tablespoon chopped sage leaves
2 teaspoons thyme leaves
sea salt and cracked black pepper
1 leek, finely sliced
4 field mushrooms, thickly sliced
¼ cup (60ml) balsamic vinegar
2 teaspoons caster (superfine) sugar
100g soft goat's cheese

Place water in a frying pan over medium-high heat and heat until bubbling. Add polenta and stir for 2–3 minutes or until creamy. Stir through 30g of the butter, parmesan, sage, thyme, salt and pepper and spoon onto heated plates. Clean pan and return to heat. Add remaining butter and leek and cook for 2 minutes. Add mushrooms and cook for a further 5–7 minutes or until golden. Stir in vinegar and sugar. Top polenta with goat's cheese and mushrooms. **SERVES 2**.

five-spice chicken & asian greens

¼ cup (60ml) dry sherry or Shaoxing wine (G)
½ cup (125ml) soy sauce
1 teaspoon Chinese five-spice powder
2 slices ginger
1 cup (250ml) chicken stock
1 tablespoon brown sugar
4 x 140g chicken thigh fillets, trimmed and halved
350g gai larn (Chinese broccoli), cut into thirds
steamed rice, to serve

Combine sherry, soy, five-spice, ginger slices, stock and sugar in a medium non-stick frying pan over high heat, bring to the boil and cook for 8–10 minutes. Add chicken and simmer for 3 minutes. Turn chicken, add gai larn stalks, cover pan and continue cooking for a further 3–5 minutes or until the chicken is cooked through. Remove chicken, add gai larn leaves to pan, cook 1 minute or until wilted. Serve chicken, sauce and gai larn on steamed rice. **SERVES 2**.

SPINACH PAN POLENTA WITH MINUTE STEAKS

PORK POTSTICKER DUMPLINGS WITH SOY GREENS

spinach pan polenta with minute steaks

3 cups (750ml) boiling water
¾ cup (120g) instant polenta
30g butter
100g baby English spinach leaves
⅓ cup (25g) finely grated parmesan
6 x 65g thinly sliced eye fillet steaks
sea salt and cracked black pepper
30g butter, extra
store-bought onion marmalade, to serve

Place water in a non-stick frying pan over medium-high heat. Add polenta, stirring constantly for 2 minutes or until polenta is cooked and creamy. Stir through butter, spinach and parmesan. Spoon the polenta into warmed shallow bowls. Clean pan and place over high heat. Sprinkle steaks well with salt and pepper. Add extra butter and steaks to the pan and cook for 30 seconds each side or until well browned. Place steaks on top of polenta and serve with onion marmalade. **SERVES 2**.

Instant polenta is a constant in my pantry. I love the fact that it so quickly transforms a simple grill or braise into a splendid meal. Think of it as you would mashed potato, with all the same smooth and comforting qualities but none of the peeling, chopping, draining and mashing that is involved with mash. Polenta readily takes on flavours so make your own signature version by adding your favourite seasonings such as herbs and cheeses.

pork potsticker dumplings with soy greens

240g pork mince
1 tablespoon hoisin sauce
2 teaspoons finely grated ginger
2 green onions (scallions), finely sliced
12 round wonton wrappers
2 teaspoons vegetable oil
½ cup (125ml) chicken stock
350g choy sum
2 tablespoons soy sauce, to serve

Combine mince, hoisin, ginger and onion. Place spoonfuls of the mixture on each wonton. Brush edges with water, fold in half and press to seal. Heat a non-stick frying pan over medium-high heat. Add oil and dumplings and cook for 2 minutes or until bases are well browned. Add stock and choy sum to the pan and cover with a tight-fitting lid. Cook for 6–8 minutes without lifting the lid. To serve, sprinkle choy sum and dumplings with soy sauce. **SERVES 2**.

sichuan beef with ginger-soy greens

1 tablespoon Sichuan peppercorns (G)
1 teaspoon sea salt flakes
400g beef fillet
1 tablespoon vegetable oil
2 teaspoons sesame oil
1 tablespoon grated ginger
350g baby bok choy
2 tablespoons soy sauce
2 tablespoons oyster sauce
1 tablespoon sugar
1 tablespoon water

Heat a medium non-stick frying pan over high heat. Add Sichuan peppercorns and salt to a pan and cook for 2–3 minutes or until fragrant. Place peppercorn mixture in a mortar and pestle and pound until fine. Sprinkle the beef on all sides with the peppercorn mix. Place oil and beef in a medium non-stick frying pan and cook for 3–4 minutes each side or until cooked to your liking. Place the beef on a warm plate and cover to keep warm. Place sesame oil and ginger in the pan and cook for 1 minute. Add bok choy to the pan and cook for 1 minute. Add combined soy, oyster sauce, sugar and water and cook for another 2–3 minutes or until the bok choy is tender. To serve, divide bok choy between plates. Slice the beef and place on top of the greens. **SERVES 2**.

SICHUAN BEEF WITH GINGER-SOY GREENS

potato & smoked salmon frittata

½ cup (120g) sour cream
1 tablespoon lemon juice
500g potatoes, peeled and diced
30g butter
¼ cup (60ml) water
4 eggs
¾ cup (180ml) cream
2 tablespoons chopped dill leaves
1 teaspoon finely grated lemon rind
sea salt and cracked black pepper
175g hot-smoked salmon fillet (G), cut into chunks

Combine sour cream and lemon juice in a small bowl, cover and refrigerate. Place potato, butter and water into a 21cm non-stick frying pan over medium heat. Cover and cook for 15 minutes or until the potatoes are soft and the liquid has evaporated. Whisk together eggs, cream, dill, lemon rind, salt and pepper. Pour over potatoes, stir once and top with salmon. Cook over low heat for 5–8 minutes or until the outside of the frittata sets. Place under a preheated grill and cook for 5–8 minutes or until frittata is golden and set through. Serve with the lemon sour cream. **SERVES 2.**

ricotta-basil chicken & wilted tomatoes

100g fresh ricotta
1 tablespoon shredded basil
1 tablespoon finely grated parmesan
2 x 200g chicken breast fillets, skin on
sea salt and cracked black pepper
1 tablespoon olive oil
250g cherry tomatoes, halved
extra basil leaves, to serve

Preheat oven to 160°C (320°F). Combine ricotta, shredded basil and parmesan. Carefully loosen the skin from the chicken breast, leaving ends intact and carefully spoon in ricotta mixture. Sprinkle chicken with salt and pepper. Heat a medium non-stick frying pan with an ovenproof handle over medium-high heat. Add oil and chicken to the pan and cook chicken for 2 minutes each side or until well browned. Add tomatoes, place the pan in the oven and cook for 10 minutes or until the chicken is cooked through. Divide between plates and top with extra basil. **SERVES 2.**

italian veal & mozzarella stack

4 x 60g thin veal steaks
40g butter
1 clove garlic, crushed
1 teaspoon lemon zest
1 tablespoon lemon juice
2 tomatoes, thickly sliced
4 slices prosciutto
1 buffalo mozzarella, torn into quarters
30g rocket (arugula) leaves
¼ cup basil leaves, torn

Place a large non-stick frying pan with an ovenproof handle over high heat, add veal and cook for 30 seconds each side or until cooked to your liking. Remove veal from pan and set aside to keep warm. Add butter, garlic, lemon zest and juice and cook until the butter melts and garlic is lightly browned. Layer veal, tomato, prosciutto, mozzarella, rocket and basil on plates, drizzle with the garlic butter. **SERVES 2**.

chicken patties with basil & cashews

1 tablespoon store-bought chilli jam or chilli jam (G)
  marinade (recipe, page 58)
350g chicken mince
4 kaffir lime leaves, shredded
1 eggwhite
1 tablespoon vegetable oil
100g snow peas (mange tout), trimmed and finely sliced
1 cup basil leaves
2 tablespoons roasted unsalted cashews, roughly chopped

Combine chilli jam, mince, lime leaves and eggwhite. Shape into 4 small patties. Heat a frying pan over medium-high heat. Add oil and patties and cook for 3–4 minutes each side or until cooked through. Add snow peas to the pan, cook for 1 minute further and stir in basil. Divide patties and snow pea mixture between serving plates and sprinkle with chopped cashews to serve. **SERVES 2**.

SPICED CHICKEN & CHORIZO COUSCOUS

DOUBLE-COOKED STICKY RIBS

spiced chicken & chorizo couscous

1 onion, coarsely chopped
1 x 200g chicken breast fillet, chopped
1 x 150g chorizo sausage, sliced
½ teaspoon chilli flakes
2 cloves garlic, sliced
1 cup (200g) instant couscous
1 cup (250ml) chicken stock
½ cup (125ml) water
100g baby English spinach leaves
1 cup (150g) pitted Kalamata olives

Place onion, chicken, chorizo, chilli and garlic into a non-stick frying pan over medium-high heat and cook for 5–6 minutes or until chicken is browned. Add couscous, stock and water to the pan, cover and simmer over low heat for 2 minutes or until couscous is tender. Stir spinach and olives through couscous mixture to serve. **SERVES 2**.

Couscous is another of those essential ingredients for any well-stocked pantry. Apart from its many guises as a side dish, it makes a great thickener for soups and stews and a fantastic base for stuffings and salads. I always prefer the instant variety for speed and ease of preparation and make it with a full-bodied chicken or vegetable stock rather than water for the extra flavour.

double-cooked sticky ribs

6 pork spare ribs
1 cinnamon stick
1 star anise
3 slices ginger
hoisin-ginger marinade
⅓ cup hoisin sauce
2 tablespoons soy sauce
2 teaspoons grated ginger
½ teaspoon Chinese five-spice powder
1 tablespoon brown sugar

Place ribs in a medium non-stick frying pan with an ovenproof handle. Add cinnamon, star anise, ginger and enough hot water to cover ribs. Place over medium heat and simmer for 20 minutes (do not allow mixture to boil). Set aside for 10 minutes. Preheat oven to 200°C (390°F). To make the marinade, combine hoisin, soy, ginger, five-spice and sugar. Drain the ribs, discarding water and flavourings and pat dry with absorbent paper. Wipe pan clean, return the ribs to pan and brush with marinade. Bake for 35 minutes or until glazed and crispy on the edges. **SERVES 2**.

cider-glazed pork cutlets

4 x 150g pork cutlets, trimmed
sea salt and cracked black pepper
1 tablespoon vegetable oil
1 clove garlic, crushed
⅓ cup sage leaves
1 cup (250ml) apple cider
¼ cup (80g) red currant jelly
2 tablespoons red wine vinegar
150g green beans, trimmed

Sprinkle pork cutlets with salt and pepper. Heat a non-stick frying pan over medium heat, add oil and pork and cook 2 minutes each side. Remove from the pan and set aside. Add garlic, sage, cider, jelly and vinegar and cook, stirring occasionally, until the mixture is reduced by half. Return cutlets to the pan, add beans and cook for a further 5 minutes or until pork is cooked through. **SERVES 2**.

CIDER-GLAZED PORK CUTLETS

lime & lemongrass salmon cakes

½ cup whole-egg mayonnaise
1½ teaspoons wasabi
1 teaspoon lime juice
2 x 180g salmon fillets, cut into 1cm cubes
1 tablespoon rice flour
1 eggwhite
1 teaspoon finely grated lime rind
1 stalk lemongrass, finely chopped
3 kaffir lime leaves, shredded
1 long red chilli, seeded and chopped
sea salt and cracked black pepper
vegetable oil, for shallow-frying
lime wedges and salad greens, to serve

Place mayonnaise, wasabi and juice in a small bowl and stir to combine. Set aside. Place salmon, rice flour, eggwhite, lime rind, lemongrass, lime leaves, chilli, salt and pepper in a bowl and mix to combine. Shape mixture into 4 patties. Heat a medium frying pan over medium heat. Add oil to the pan, add patties and cook for 4 minutes each side or until cooked through. Serve with lime wedges, salad greens and lime and wasabi mayonnaise. **SERVES 2.**

coriander & coconut poached chicken

2 x 200g chicken breast fillets, halved lengthways
6 thin slices peeled pumpkin (420g trimmed)
1 cup (250ml) coconut milk
4 kaffir lime leaves
1 long red chilli, halved
3 slices ginger
1 tablespoon fish sauce
150g snow peas (mange tout), trimmed
coriander (cilantro) leaves, to serve
steamed rice, to serve
lime cheeks, to serve

Heat a non-stick frying pan over medium–high heat. Add chicken and cook for 1 minute each side or until light golden. Add pumpkin, coconut milk, lime leaves, chilli, ginger and fish sauce and simmer for 8–10 minutes or until pumpkin is tender. Add snow peas and cook for 1 minute. Sprinkle with coriander and serve with steamed rice and lime cheeks. **SERVES 2.**

thai ginger chicken salad

2 teaspoons vegetable oil

350g chicken mince

½ teaspoon chilli flakes

4 kaffir lime leaves, shredded, optional

2 tablespoons lime juice

2 tablespoons fish sauce

1 tablespoon brown sugar

1 cup mint leaves

2 tablespoons vegetable oil, extra

2 tablespoons shredded ginger

crisp lettuce leaves and lime wedges, to serve

Heat a medium non-stick frying pan over medium–high heat. Add oil, mince and chilli and cook, stirring, for 5 minutes or until mince is cooked through. Stir through lime leaves and juice, fish sauce and sugar and cook for 1 minute. Remove from heat and stir through mint. Divide between serving plates. Wipe out pan and place over high heat. Add extra oil and ginger to the pan and cook until ginger is crisp. Drain on absorbent paper and sprinkle over the chicken. Serve with lettuce and lime. **SERVES 2**.

wasabi salmon with mushy peas

2 x 200g salmon fillets

2 teaspoons wasabi

2 sheets nori (G)

olive oil, for brushing

2 cups (240g) frozen peas

40g butter

sea salt and cracked black pepper

1 green onion (scallion), finely sliced

coriander (cilantro) leaves, to serve

Brush salmon with wasabi, wrap in nori, trim edges and brush lightly with olive oil. Heat a medium non-stick frying pan over medium–high heat, cook salmon 4–5 minutes each side, or until cooked to your liking. Pour boiling water over the peas, stand for 3 minutes, drain. Use a potato masher or stick mixer to mash peas with butter, salt and pepper until just combined and stir through onion. Divide the pea mixture between plates, top with salmon and sprinkle with coriander to serve. **SERVES 2**.

BALSAMIC CHICKEN STACK

SMOKY BAKED BEANS

balsamic chicken stack

½ cup (125ml) balsamic vinegar
1 tablespoon oregano leaves
2 tablespoons brown sugar
½ teaspoon cracked black pepper
2 x 200g chicken breast fillets, halved lengthways
1 tomato, sliced
1 large fresh mozzarella, halved
⅓ cup basil leaves
olive oil, for drizzling

Place vinegar, oregano, sugar and pepper in a medium non-stick frying pan over medium heat and cook for 3–4 minutes or until the liquid has thickened slightly. Add chicken and cook for 3 minutes each side or until cooked through. Place chicken on serving plates. Divide tomatoes, mozzarella and basil between the plates. Drizzle with a little oil and serve. **SERVES 2**.

This recipe has followed me right through my career, ever since I first published it in one of my earliest columns for a fashion magazine. It speaks volumes that it's still my standby for those many times when I need something special for dinner and fast. We've tweaked the ingredients a little, using the wonderful fresh mozzarella that's now available, but the essence of bold flavours that come together in minutes remains the same.

smoky baked beans

1 onion, chopped
2 x 150g chorizo sausages, chopped
400g can butter or Lima beans, drained and rinsed
400ml tomato passata (G)
½ cup (125ml) beef stock
½ teaspoon smoked sweet paprika
½ cup flatleaf parsley leaves
cracked black pepper
buttered toast, to serve

Heat a medium frying pan over high heat. Add onion and chorizo and cook for 5 minutes or until well browned. Add beans, passata, stock and paprika and simmer for 7–8 minutes. Stir in parsley and pepper and serve with toast. **SERVES 2**.

spiced fish with sesame-ginger noodles

1 teaspoon sesame oil
1 tablespoon sesame seeds
1 tablespoon grated ginger
3 green onions (scallions), sliced
1 tablespoon fish sauce
100g dried rice stick noodles
2 teaspoons red curry paste
1 tablespoon olive oil
2 x 200g firm white fish fillets
⅓ cup coriander (cilantro) leaves
⅓ cup mint leaves

Place a medium non-stick frying pan over low heat, add sesame oil, seeds, ginger, onion and fish sauce and cook for 2–3 minutes. Remove sesame mixture from pan and set aside. Wipe pan clean. Place noodles in a heatproof bowl, cover with boiling water for 10 minutes, or until separated and tender. Combine curry paste and oil in a bowl and brush over the fish. Return the pan to low heat, add fish and cook for 5 minutes each side or until the fish is cooked through. Drain noodles, stir through sesame mixture and divide between plates. Top with fish and herbs to serve. **SERVES 2**.

SPICED FISH WITH SESAME-GINGER NOODLES

rustic simmered chicken

2 tablespoons olive oil
1 leek, trimmed and chopped
2 cloves garlic, sliced
4 slices pancetta, chopped
4 x 140g chicken thigh fillets, halved
plain (all-purpose) flour, for dusting
200g small button mushrooms
4 chat (baby) potatoes, quartered
½ cup (125ml) dry white wine
1 cup (250ml) chicken stock
3 sprigs thyme
1 sprig tarragon
½ cup (125ml) cream
sea salt and cracked black pepper

Heat a frying pan over medium-high heat. Add oil, leek, garlic and pancetta and cook for 1 minute or until golden. Dust chicken with flour and cook for 2 minutes each side or until golden. Add mushrooms, cook for 2 minutes. Add potatoes, wine, stock, thyme and tarragon, reduce heat, cover and simmer for 25–30 minutes or until chicken is tender. Stir in cream, salt and pepper. **SERVES 2.**

creamy spinach & pancetta eggs

4 slices pancetta, roughly chopped
100g baby English spinach leaves
4 eggs
¾ cup (180ml) cream
sea salt and cracked black pepper
30g butter
1 teaspoon finely grated lemon rind
finely grated parmesan, to serve
buttered toast, to serve

Heat a medium non-stick frying pan over medium-high heat. Add pancetta and cook for 3 minutes, then add spinach and cook for 1–2 minutes or until just wilted. Set the spinach mixture aside. Wipe out pan and return to heat. Whisk together eggs, cream, salt and pepper. Place butter in the pan and heat until melted. Add egg mixture and gently move around the pan until egg is just set. Fold through the spinach mixture. Sprinkle with lemon rind and serve with parmesan and toast. **SERVES 2.**

spinach, ricotta & bacon frittata

4 rashers bacon, rind removed and chopped
100g baby English spinach leaves
4 eggs
½ cup (125ml) milk
½ cup (125ml) cream
sea salt and cracked black pepper
180g fresh ricotta
buttered toast, to serve

Place a small non-stick frying pan with an ovenproof handle over medium–high heat. Add bacon and cook for 4 minutes or until lightly browned. Add spinach and cook for 1–2 minutes or until wilted. Whisk together eggs, milk, cream, salt and pepper. Pour mixture into the pan and stir to evenly distribute the bacon and spinach through the eggs. Drop spoonfuls of ricotta over the frittata. Cook over low heat for 5–8 minutes or until the outside of the frittata is set. Place under a preheated grill and cook for 5–8 minutes or until frittata is golden and set. Serve in wedges with hot buttered toast. **SERVES 2**.

fennel-crusted pork

2 teaspoons fennel seeds
1 teaspoon sea salt flakes
¼ teaspoon cracked black pepper
2 teaspoons roughly chopped rosemary leaves
375g pork fillet, trimmed
2 teaspoons olive oil
30g butter
1 tablespoon white wine vinegar
2 teaspoons brown sugar
400g white cabbage, shredded
1 green apple, grated

Place fennel, salt, pepper and rosemary in a mortar and pestle and pound to a coarse mixture. Sprinkle fennel mixture over pork. Heat a non-stick frying pan over medium–high heat. Add oil and pork and cook for 4 minutes each side, or until the pork is cooked to your liking. Remove from pan, place on a warm plate and cover to keep warm. Wipe out pan and return to the heat. Place butter, vinegar and sugar in the pan and cook until the butter is melted and the sugar is dissolved. Add cabbage and apple, cook, stirring, until the cabbage is wilted. Serve with the sliced pork. **SERVES 2**.

CHEATS 3.

salad sides

If you want your meal to make a statement
you have to be sure to team it with the right
accessories. Just as a basic outfit becomes
signature style when matched with the right
shoes and jewellery, a perfectly composed salad
can elevate a simple grill or roast from plain
to peerless. Use only the freshest ingredients
and stand back for the oohs and aahs.

mint & zucchini salad with caramelised lemon

RIGHT: Cut 4 zucchini (courgette) into fine ribbons using a vegetable peeler. Toss with ½ cup roughly chopped mint leaves, 1 tablespoon olive oil, sea salt and cracked black pepper. Halve a lemon and place flesh side down in a hot non-stick frying pan and cook for 3 minutes or until lemon is golden. Squeeze the caramelised lemon over the salad and serve with shaved parmesan. **SERVES 4.**

rocket, fig & prosciutto salad

BELOW: Place 4 slices of prosciutto onto a board. Top each slice with a small bundle of rocket (arugula) leaves, half a fig and sliced buffalo or cow's milk mozzarella. Sprinkle with a good quality balsamic vinegar, extra virgin olive oil, sea salt flakes and a generous quantity of cracked black pepper. Fold over the slices of prosciutto to enclose the filling before serving. **SERVES 4.**

Basic salad ingredients radiate when paired with the right dressing. Caramelised lemon slices reinvent the humble zucchini while a classic basil and tomato combo is transformed with a twist.

basil-spiked tomatoes

ABOVE: Cut a cross almost through 4 ox heart or heirloom tomatoes. Fill each incision with 2 sprigs basil and sprinkle with salt and pepper. Combine ¾ cup (180ml) of olive oil and ½ cup of basil leaves in a pan over low heat and cook for 5 minutes or to just warm the olive oil. Set aside for 15 minutes and strain, reserving the infused oil. Place 1 cup of extra blanched basil leaves and 1½ tablespoons extra olive oil in blender and process to a paste. Stir paste into basil oil. Drizzle over tomatoes. **SERVES 4.**

snow pea salad

LEFT: Blanch 250g snow peas (mange tout) in boiling water for 1 minute. Drain, refresh under cold water and place in a bowl with 30g snow pea shoots and 1 finely sliced long red chilli. Mix together 2 tablespoons soy sauce, 1 tablespoon lemon juice and 2 tablespoons brown sugar. Pour the soy dressing over the snow pea mixture to serve. **SERVES 4.**

spinach with sesame miso dressing

RIGHT: Combine 2 tablespoons white miso paste (**G**) with ½ teaspoon sesame oil, 2 teaspoons brown sugar, ¼ cup (60ml) water, 1 tablespoon toasted sesame seeds and a finely sliced green onion (scallion). Pour the dressing over 150g baby spinach or crisp salad leaves to serve. This dressing is also great when spooned over grilled chicken, tofu, vegetables or seafood. **SERVES 4.**

mint and avocado couscous salad

BELOW: Place 1 cup (200g) couscous into a small heatproof bowl. Pour over 1¼ cups (310ml) hot chicken stock and top with 30g butter. Cover tightly with plastic wrap and stand for 5 minutes or until stock is absorbed. Add 1 cup torn mint leaves, a quartered avocado and 2 tablespoons lightly toasted pine nuts. Combine 1 tablespoon honey with 2 tablespoons lemon juice, sea salt and cracked black pepper, and pour over salad. **SERVES 4.**

As basic as a salad's inspiration may be, it's the combination of ingredients that can lift it from simple to sublime. Different textures and flavours make for happy pairings on the plate.

herbed risoni salad

ABOVE: Cook 1 cup (220g) risoni in salted boiling water until al dente, drain and rinse under cold water. Combine the cooked risoni with 2 tablespoons olive oil, 1 tablespoon lemon juice, ½ cup roughly chopped parsley leaves, ½ cup roughly chopped mint leaves, 1 tablespoon roughly chopped dill leaves, sea salt flakes and cracked black pepper. Serve as a side to grilled or barbecued meats, fish and chicken. **SERVES 4.**

spiced chickpea & carrot salad

LEFT: Heat 2 tablespoons of olive oil in a small frying pan over medium heat. Add 2 cloves crushed garlic, 1 teaspoon ground cumin, 1 teaspoon ground coriander (cilantro) and 1 teaspoon smoked paprika. Cook for 1 minute then pour spice mixture over a 400g can of drained and rinsed chickpeas (garbanzos). Toss chickpea mixture with 2 coarsely grated carrots, 1 tablespoon white wine vinegar and 1 tablespoon honey. **SERVES 4.**

lettuce with buttermilk dressing

RIGHT: Place ⅓ cup (80ml) buttermilk, ⅓ cup (95g) natural thick yoghurt, 1 crushed clove garlic, 2 tablespoons chopped chives, salt and pepper in a bowl and whisk to combine. To serve, spoon dressing over wedges of iceberg lettuce or any crisp salad leaves. This dressing also goes with coleslaw. **SERVES 4.**

fennel, parsley & feta salad

BELOW: Finely slice 2 trimmed fennel bulbs and place on a serving plate. Combine 2 tablespoons apple cider vinegar with 2 tablespoons olive oil, sea salt and cracked black pepper and pour dressing over the fennel. Sprinkle with ¾ cup flatleaf parsley leaves. Top with 200g crumbled feta to serve. **SERVES 4.**

There's something irresistible about the marriage of crunchy greens and a creamy dressing or crumbling of cheese. Tahini, too, can give an inspired lift to time-honoured salads.

marinated celery & goat's cheese salad

ABOVE: Use a vegetable peeler to thinly slice 6 stalks of celery into ribbons and place celery in a bowl with ¼ cup (60ml) lemon juice and 2 tablespoons roughly chopped dill sprigs and allow to stand for 10 minutes. Sprinkle with olive oil, sea salt and cracked black pepper and top with slices of firm goat's cheese. **SERVES 4.**

cucumber salad with tahini dressing

LEFT: Place 2 sliced Lebanese cucumbers, 60g baby English spinach leaves and 2 tablespoons roughly torn mint leaves into serving bowls. Place ¼ cup (70g) tahini, ¼ cup (60ml) water, ¼ cup (60ml) lemon juice, 1 clove crushed garlic, sea salt and cracked black pepper in a bowl and whisk well to combine. Pour over the cucumber salad to serve. **SERVES 4.**

ONE POT

Cooking is a great way to unwind at the end
of the day but tackling the washing of the pots
and pans after turning out your gastronomic
sensation is yet another story entirely. Wave
goodbye to mountains of washing up with these
recipes that use just one pot to create meals that
are hearty and full of flavour but leave
you with a bare minimum of cleaning up.

SQUASHED CHERRY TOMATO SPAGHETTI

CREAMY POTATO & PORCINI SOUP

squashed cherry tomato spaghetti

200g spaghetti
olive oil, for drizzling
30g butter
2 cloves garlic, crushed
2 tablespoons balsamic vinegar
500g cherry tomatoes
1 cup torn basil leaves
finely grated parmesan, to serve

Cook spaghetti in a large saucepan of salted boiling water
for 10-12 minutes or until al dente. Drain, drizzle with olive oil
and set aside to keep warm. Return pan to the heat and cook
butter, garlic, vinegar and tomatoes for 4 minutes or until the
tomatoes are heated through and slightly soft. Add spaghetti
to the tomato mixture and toss through basil leaves. Sprinkle
with parmesan to serve. SERVES 2.

*Cherry and grape tomatoes have an extended
ripening season so they often have a sweeter
flavour than the larger vine tomato varieties.
By squeezing the seeds from cherry tomatoes
you remove the watery juice and sometimes
bitter taste of the seeds and further intensify
their delicious, fresh flavour.*

creamy potato & porcini soup

25g dried porcini mushrooms (G)
1½ cups (375ml) boiling water
1 tablespoon olive oil
1 leek, chopped
3 sprigs thyme
750g floury (starchy) potatoes, peeled and finely chopped
1 litre chicken stock
¼ cup (60ml) cream
sea salt and cracked black pepper
thick slices toasted sourdough, to serve
finely grated parmesan, to serve

Place dried porcini in a heatproof bowl, cover with boiling water
and stand for 10 minutes. Drain porcini, reserving 1 cup (250ml)
soaking liquid. Finely slice porcini. Place saucepan over medium
heat, add oil, leek and thyme and cook for 5 minutes, or until
leek is soft and golden. Increase heat to high, add sliced porcini,
potato, stock and reserved soaking liquid. Cook for 30-35 minutes
or until the potatoes begin to break up and naturally thicken
the soup. Remove thyme sprigs and stir in cream, salt and pepper.
Serve with thick slices of sourdough toast and parmesan. SERVES 2.

pappardelle carbonara

200g pappardelle
2 egg yolks
¾ cup (180ml) cream
⅓ cup (25g) finely grated parmesan
cracked black pepper
4 slices prosciutto
extra grated parmesan, to serve

Cook pappardelle in a large saucepan of salted boiling water
for 10-12 minutes or until al dente. Drain, return pasta to the
pan and place over very low heat. Combine egg yolks, cream,
parmesan and pepper, pour over pasta, return to heat and toss
to coat for 1-2 minutes or until the sauce thickens slightly. Divide
pasta between serving bowls and top with prosciutto and the
extra parmesan to serve. SERVES 2.

PAPPARDELLE CARBONARA

chinese chicken hotpot

2 ½ cups (625ml) chicken stock

3 slices ginger

3 cloves garlic, bruised and peeled

1 ¼ cups (250g) jasmine rice

3 x 140g chicken thigh fillets, halved

100g snow peas (mange tout), trimmed

soy sauce, to serve

onion-ginger dressing

1 green onion (scallion), trimmed and finely sliced

1 tablespoon finely grated ginger

2 tablespoons vegetable oil

2 tablespoons chopped coriander (cilantro) leaves

½ teaspoon sea salt flakes

To make onion-ginger dressing, combine all ingredients in a small bowl and set aside. Combine stock, ginger and garlic in a medium pot and bring to the boil. Add rice, return to the boil. Top with the chicken and cover with a tight-fitting lid. Cook for 10 minutes over low heat. Remove pot from heat, add the snow peas and allow to stand for 5 minutes or until all the liquid has been absorbed. Spoon over the onion-ginger dressing, soy sauce and serve. **SERVES 2.**

pork & sweet potato red curry

1 tablespoon vegetable oil

1 ½ tablespoons Thai red curry paste

1 onion, cut into wedges

2 teaspoons grated ginger

250g orange sweet potato (kumara), thinly sliced

1 cup (250ml) coconut milk

1 cup (250ml) chicken stock

350g pork fillet, sliced thinly

½ cup basil leaves

½ cup coriander (cilantro) leaves

Heat oil in a medium saucepan over medium–high heat. Add curry paste and cook for 1 minute or until fragrant. Add onion and ginger and cook for 2 minutes. Add potato, coconut milk and stock and simmer for 8 minutes or until the potato is just soft. Add pork to the pan and cook for 4 minutes or until just cooked through. Spoon the curry into serving bowls and top with basil and coriander. **SERVES 2.**

chilli vinegar crispy fish with noodles

300g fresh wide rice noodles
vegetable oil, for deep-frying
350g firm white fish, cut into pieces
½ cup (100g) rice flour
½ teaspoon Chinese five-spice powder
½ cup coriander (cilantro) leaves
soy sauce, to serve
chilli vinegar
½ cup (125ml) white vinegar
½ cup (110g) sugar
3 long red chillies, sliced
1 tablespoon shredded ginger

To make chilli vinegar, place vinegar, sugar, chilli and ginger in a pan over medium heat and cook for 8–10 minutes or until syrupy, pour into a bowl and set aside. Place noodles in a bowl, cover with boiling water and stir to separate. Drain and set aside. Rinse and dry pan, fill a third full with oil and return to medium heat. Toss fish in combined rice flour and five-spice. Deep-fry fish in batches until crisp and cooked through, drain. Sprinkle noodles with coriander and soy and top with fish and chilli vinegar. **SERVES 2**.

lemongrass chicken wonton soup

200g chicken mince
1 stalk lemongrass, finely chopped
2 teaspoons finely grated ginger
1 eggwhite
12 wonton wrappers
1 litre chicken stock
2 slices ginger
2 kaffir lime leaves, crushed
1 long red chilli, sliced
350g gai larn (Chinese broccoli)

Combine mince, lemongrass, ginger and eggwhite. Place a tablespoon of chicken mixture onto each wonton wrapper. Brush the edges of the wrapper with water, fold in half and press edges together to enclose filling. Place stock, ginger, lime leaves and chilli in a saucepan over medium-high heat and bring to a simmer. Add wontons and simmer for 6 minutes or until the wontons are almost cooked. Add gai larn and cook for a further 2 minutes. Divide wontons between bowls, serve with soup and gai larn. **SERVES 2**.

POTATO & CHICKEN SALAD WITH SALSA VERDE

PENNE WITH ROCKET, PARMESAN & OLIVES

potato & chicken salad with salsa verde

6 kipfler potatoes
1 sprig mint
2 x 200g cooked chicken breasts, shredded
1 tablespoon salted capers, rinsed
60g baby rocket (arugula) leaves
salsa verde
1 cup flatleaf parsley leaves
1 cup mint leaves
½ cup dill sprigs
¼ cup (60ml) olive oil
1 tablespoon Dijon mustard
1 tablespoon lemon juice
cracked black pepper

To make the salsa verde, place parsley, mint, dill, oil, mustard, lemon juice and pepper into a food processor and process the mixture in bursts until roughly chopped. Place potatoes and mint in a saucepan of water and boil for 15 minutes or until potatoes are tender. Drain and discard mint. Halve potatoes and return to the warm saucepan with chicken and capers and gently toss over low heat to warm. Toss the salsa through the potato and chicken mixture. Divide the rocket between serving bowls and top with the chicken and potato salad. SERVES 2.

Salsa verde is a wonderful stand-by to have in the fridge as it gives a fast injection of flavour to all manner of dishes. Stir it through hot pasta or use it as an instant accompaniment for grilled or roasted fish, chicken, lamb or vegies. Best of all, you can make it well in advance and keep it in the fridge for up to a week.

penne with rocket, parmesan & olives

200g penne
1½ tablespoons olive oil
2 cloves garlic, crushed
2 anchovies, chopped
½ cup (60g) small pitted back olives, chopped
1 teaspoon finely grated lemon rind
2 cups shredded rocket (arugula) leaves
½ cup (40g) finely grated parmesan, to serve

Cook pasta in a large saucepan of salted boiling water for 10-12 minutes or until al dente. Drain and set aside. Return pan to heat. Add oil, garlic, anchovies, olives and lemon rind and cook for 2 minutes. Return the pasta to the pan and toss to combine. Add rocket and toss. Divide penne between bowls and top with grated parmesan to serve. SERVES 2.

pancetta, sage & ricotta pasta

200g rigatoni or short pasta
15g butter
1 teaspoon olive oil
8 sage leaves
8 slices pancetta, sliced thickly
½ cup (60g) halved green olives
pinch chilli flakes
1 tablespoon lemon zest
2 tablespoons lemon juice
150g fresh ricotta
finely grated parmesan, to serve

Cook pasta in a large saucepan of salted boiling water for 10-12 minutes or until al dente. Drain and set aside. Return pan to the heat. Add butter, oil, sage and pancetta and cook for 3 minutes or until the pancetta is crisp. Add olives, chilli, lemon zest and juice and pasta to the pan and toss to coat. Place pasta in serving bowls, top with spoonfuls of ricotta and sprinkle with grated parmesan. SERVES 2.

PANCETTA, SAGE & RICOTTA PASTA

shredded rocket & prawn linguine

200g linguine
2 tablespoons olive oil
4 cloves garlic
12 green (raw) prawns (shrimp), peeled and halved
1 teaspoon lemon zest
½ teaspoon chilli flakes
sea salt and cracked black pepper
50g rocket (arugula) leaves, shredded
squeeze lemon juice

Cook linguine in a large saucepan of salted boiling water for 10–12 minutes or until al dente. Drain and set aside to keep warm. Return the saucepan to medium-high heat, add olive oil, garlic, prawns, lemon zest, chilli, salt and pepper and cook for 2 minutes, or until the prawns are just cooked and pink. Toss prawn mixture through spaghetti with rocket and lemon juice and serve immediately. **SERVES 2.**

garlic & tomato fish stew

1 tablespoon olive oil
4 cloves garlic, crushed
1 teaspoon finely grated lemon rind
½ onion, finely sliced
½ cup (125ml) dry white wine
½ cup (125ml) fish or vegetable stock
400g can peeled tomatoes, crushed
6 chat (baby) potatoes, quartered
350g firm white fish, cut into large pieces
sea salt and cracked black pepper
⅓ cup flatleaf parsley leaves, torn
crusty bread, to serve

Heat a medium saucepan over medium heat. Add oil, garlic, lemon rind and onion and cook for 2 minutes or until the onion is just soft. Add wine and cook for 3 minutes. Add stock, tomato and potato, cover and simmer for 8 minutes. Add fish, salt and pepper and cook for 4 minutes or until the fish is cooked through. Spoon into bowls and top with parsley. Serve with bread. **SERVES 2.**

gnocchi with lemon & wilted rocket

450g potato gnocchi
½ cup (125ml) cream
1 tablespoon lemon juice
2 teaspoons grated lemon rind
2 cups shredded rocket (arugula) leaves
sea salt and cracked black pepper
finely grated parmesan, to serve

Place gnocchi into a saucepan of salted boiling water and cook until tender. Drain and set aside to keep warm. Return saucepan to the heat and add cream, lemon juice and rind. Toss through rocket, salt, pepper and the drained gnocchi. Divide gnocchi and sauce between serving plates and sprinkle with finely grated parmesan to serve. SERVES 2.

chilli jam prawns with thai rice

1½ cups (300g) jasmine rice
2¼ cups (560ml) water
½ cup (125ml) coconut milk
1 stalk lemongrass, trimmed and finely sliced
1 tablespoon grated ginger
3 kaffir lime leaves, shredded
sea salt
12 green (raw) prawns (shrimp), heads and shells removed
2 teaspoons grated ginger
2 tablespoons chilli jam (G)
coriander (cilantro) leaves and lime wedges, to serve

Place rice, water, coconut milk, lemongrass, ginger, lime leaves and salt in a saucepan over medium heat. Bring to the boil and cook for 12 minutes or until tunnels form in the rice and most of the liquid has been absorbed. Toss prawns in ginger and chilli jam and place on top of the rice. Cover and cook for 2 minutes. Remove from heat, do not remove the lid but stand, covered, for another 3 minutes. Serve prawns and rice with coriander leaves and lime wedges. SERVES 2.

THREE-CHEESE RAVIOLI WITH BUTTERED SPINACH

LAMB CUTLETS WITH INDIAN-SPICED RICE

three-cheese ravioli with buttered spinach

170g fresh ricotta
½ cup (60g) grated gruyère
½ cup (40g) finely grated parmesan
1 egg yolk
cracked black pepper
2 tablespoons chopped chives
24 wonton wrappers
30g butter
1 clove garlic, crushed
200g baby spinach leaves
¼ cup (20g) flaked almonds, toasted
olive oil, for drizzling
extra finely grated parmesan, to serve

Place ricotta, gruyère, parmesan, egg yolk, pepper and chives in a bowl and stir to combine. Place tablespoons of mixture onto half the wontons. Brush the edges with water, top with remaining wontons and press together to seal. Heat a medium saucepan of salted boiling water over medium–high heat and cook ravioli for 3 minutes or until the ravioli float to the surface and are tender. Drain and set aside. Return the saucepan to the heat, add butter and garlic and cook for 1 minute more. Add spinach to the pan and cook, stirring, for a further 1 minute or until leaves are wilted. Place spinach on serving plates, sprinkle over almonds, top with ravioli and drizzle with oil. Serve with extra parmesan. **SERVES 2.**

Wonton wrappers are a great multi-function ingredient. They take all the angst out of rolling and folding pasta to make ravioli and tortellini and can be deep-fried to make a crunchy sweet or savoury base, or baked in mini-muffin tins to make little cups for canapés. Be sure to buy egg wrappers for their superior texture and flavour.

lamb cutlets with indian-spiced rice

2 tablespoons store-bought tandoori paste
6 lamb cutlets
1 tablespoon olive oil
spiced rice
1 tablespoon olive oil
1 onion, cut into wedges
2 cloves garlic, sliced
½ teaspoon cumin seeds
2 cardamom pods, crushed
1 cup (200g) long-grain rice
1¾ cups (430ml) chicken stock
¼ cup (35g) toasted slivered almonds
sea salt
¼ cup chopped coriander (cilantro) leaves
lime pickle and store-bought tzatziki, to serve

Heat a saucepan over medium–high heat. Spread tandoori paste over lamb cutlets. Add ½ tablespoon of oil to the pan and 3 cutlets and cook for 1 minute each side or until browned. Repeat with remaining cutlets and oil, place on a plate and cover to keep warm. To make spiced rice, rinse out pan and then heat over medium heat. Add oil, onion, garlic, cumin and cardamom and cook for 1 minute or until fragrant. Add rice and cook for 1 minute. Add stock and cook until tunnels form in the rice. Place cutlets on top of rice, cover pan with a tight-fitting lid and cook on very low heat for 2 minutes, remove from the heat and stand for 3 minutes. To serve, stir almonds, salt and coriander through the rice and divide between serving plates. Top with the cutlets and serve with lime pickle and tzatziki. **SERVES 2.**

lemon salmon pasta

200g thin spaghetti
¼ cup (60ml) cream
2 tablespoons lemon juice
2 teaspoons Dijon mustard
1 tablespoon roughly chopped dill
1 tablespoon salted capers, rinsed
175g hot-smoked salmon fillet, flaked

Cook spaghetti in a large saucepan of salted boiling water for 10–12 minutes or until al dente. Drain and return to the pan. Add cream, lemon juice and mustard to pasta, toss to coat. Toss through dill, capers and salmon, and serve immediately. **SERVES 2.**

LEMON SALMON PASTA

perfect pot roast chicken

1.5kg chicken
1 head garlic, halved
6 chat (baby) potatoes
12 sprigs lemon thyme
¾ cup (180ml) chicken stock
¼ cup (60ml) dry white wine
sea salt and cracked black pepper

Preheat oven to 160°C (320°F). Place chicken breast-side up in a deep-sided pot with a tight-fitting lid. Add garlic, potatoes, thyme, stock and wine. Sprinkle with salt and pepper and cover with the lid. Bake for 1 hour, then remove the lid and bake for a further 15 minutes or until chicken is golden. Carve the chicken and serve with the roasted potatoes, garlic and some of the pan juices. **SERVES 2 WITH LEFTOVER CHICKEN.**

celeriac soup with sage brown butter

2 teaspoons olive oil
1 onion, chopped
200g potatoes, peeled and chopped
500g celeriac, peeled and chopped
3 cups (750ml) chicken or vegetable stock
½ cup (125ml) cream
sea salt and cracked black pepper
sage brown butter
30g butter
8 sage leaves

Heat a saucepan over medium–high heat. Add oil and onion and cook for 3 minutes or until soft. Add potato, celeriac and stock and bring to the boil. Cover and simmer for 15 minutes or until vegetables are soft. Remove from heat and stir through cream, salt and pepper. Using a stick blender purée the soup. Spoon into serving bowls. To make sage brown butter, wash out the pot and place back over the heat. Add butter and sage and cook until the butter is golden and the sage is crisp. Spoon sage butter over the soup and serve immediately. **SERVES 2.**

broccoli, almond & lemon pasta

200g orecchiette or other short pasta
30g butter
2 cloves garlic, crushed
1 teaspoon grated lemon rind
200g small broccoli florets
1 tablespoon lemon juice
¼ cup (60ml) chicken or vegetable stock
sea salt and cracked black pepper
¼ cup (35g) slivered almonds, toasted, to serve
finely grated parmesan, to serve

Cook orecchiette in a large saucepan of salted boiling water for 10–12 minutes or until al dente. Drain and set aside. Return pan to the heat, add butter, garlic and lemon rind and cook for 1 minute. Add broccoli and cook for 3–4 minutes or until the broccoli is just tender. Add lemon juice, stock, salt, pepper and pasta and toss to combine. Divide between serving bowls and top with almonds and grated parmesan to serve. **SERVES 2.**

pumpkin & chickpea curry

1 tablespoon vegetable oil
1 red onion, sliced
2 tablespoons red curry paste
400g can chickpeas (garbanzos), drained
600g pumpkin, peeled and chopped
230g eggplant (aubergine), chopped
400ml coconut milk
1 cup (250ml) vegetable stock
1 cup basil leaves
lime wedges and steamed rice, to serve

Heat oil in saucepan over medium-high heat. Add onion and curry paste and cook for 2 minutes, or until onion softens. Add chickpeas, pumpkin, eggplant, coconut milk and vegetable stock to pot. Simmer until pumpkin is soft. Add basil and serve with lime wedges and steamed rice. **SERVES 2.**

SQUID WITH CRISPY HERBS & LEEK

PASTA WITH SUMMER HERBS

squid with crispy herbs & leek

vegetable oil, for deep-frying
1 leek, cut into long strips
¼ cup mint leaves
¼ cup basil leaves
½ cup (100g) rice flour
2 teaspoons Chinese five-spice powder
½ teaspoon sea salt
8 small cleaned squid (750g), cut into strips
green salad and aïoli, to serve

Heat oil in a deep saucepan over medium–high heat until hot.
Fry leek, mint and basil, in batches, for 15–20 seconds, or until
crispy and drain on absorbent paper. Combine flour, five-spice
and salt in a large bowl, add squid and toss to coat. Shake off
excess flour and deep-fry squid, in batches, for 1–2 minutes or
until cooked through and crispy. Drain on absorbent paper.
Divide salad between serving plates, top with squid, leek, mint
and basil and serve with aïoli. SERVES 2.

*Rice flour is a secret weapon when you want
deep-fried food to stay crunchy. The starch
component of the rice creates a particularly
serendipitous reaction when frying, which
keeps the squid extra crispy. The deep-fried
leek and whole herbs add a subtle flavour
boost as well as colour and extra crunch.*

pasta with summer herbs

200g linguine or spaghetti
30g butter
2 cloves garlic, crushed
1 cup (70g) fresh breadcrumbs
½ cup torn mint leaves
½ cup torn basil leaves
½ cup torn flatleaf parsley leaves
1 tablespoon olive oil
sea salt and cracked black pepper

Cook pasta in a large saucepan of salted boiling water for
10–12 minutes or until al dente. Drain and set aside. Return the
saucepan to the heat and add butter, garlic and breadcrumbs.
Cook, stirring, for 2 minutes or until the crumbs become golden.
Toss through pasta with herbs, oil, salt and pepper. SERVES 2.

zucchini & mint pasta

200g spaghetti
2 zucchini (courgette), grated
2 tablespoons chopped mint
1 tablespoon lemon juice
pinch chilli flakes
sea salt and cracked black pepper
finely grated parmesan, to serve

Cook pasta in a large saucepan of salted boiling water for
10–12 minutes or until al dente. Drain and return to the pan
to keep warm. Toss spaghetti with zucchini, mint, lemon juice,
chilli, salt and pepper. Divide spaghetti mixture between the
serving plates, sprinkle with finely grated parmesan and serve
immediately. SERVES 2.

ZUCCHINI & MINT PASTA

CHEATS 4.

sauces & salsas

Just as the self-help manuals keep telling us, life is all about balance. That applies as much to what's on the plate as it does to work and play. If something seems amiss, perhaps you should be thinking about adding a burst of fresh herb flavour, a rich and creamy enrobing sauce or a salsa with a tangy zing. Chances are you'll find the solution with these simple short orders.

balsamic onions

RIGHT: Cut 3 onions into wedges and place in a frying pan with a little olive oil and a few sprigs of thyme over medium–high heat. Cook for 8 minutes or until soft. Add ¼ cup (60ml) balsamic vinegar and ¼ cup (55g) caster (superfine) sugar and cook for a further 12 minutes or until onions are soft and syrupy. Serve with beef, chicken, pork or lamb.

red wine glaze

BELOW: Place 1 litre beef stock, ¼ cup (60ml) red wine and ¾ cup (240g) redcurrant jelly in a medium frying pan over high heat and bring to the boil. Reduce heat and simmer for 15 minutes or until the glaze reduces and thickens slightly. Serve red wine glaze with roasted, pan-fried or grilled beef, lamb, pork or veal.

Meat's dense texture and strong flavour sometimes needs a companion to cut through the richness. Time to call in the acidic cavalry... balsamic or cider vinegars or red and white wine rally to the rescue.

mint glaze

ABOVE: Combine ¾ cup (180ml) cider vinegar, ⅓ cup (75g) sugar and 2 tablespoons seed mustard in a frying pan over medium heat and simmer until mixture is syrupy. Remove from heat and stir through ⅓ cup shredded mint leaves, salt and pepper. Serve mint glaze with slices of roast lamb, chops and cutlets. The glaze is also great when served cold on lamb sandwiches or rolls.

herb brown butter

LEFT: Place 100g butter in a small saucepan over high heat and cook for 4–5 minutes or until nut brown. Add 12 sage leaves or ¼ cup oregano leaves, sea salt flakes and cracked black pepper and cook until the leaves are crispy. Serve herb brown butter as a condiment for soup, risotto, soft polenta, simple pastas or with grilled meats, mushrooms and other vegetables.

sweet lemon salsa

RIGHT: Peel and slice 3 lemons, making sure you remove the white pith. Place in a glass or ceramic bowl with ⅓ cup (75g) caster (superfine) sugar, ½ cup flatleaf parsley leaves and 1 tablespoon well-rinsed salted capers. Toss gently to combine and stand for 10 minutes before serving. Serve salsa with grilled, barbecued or roasted fish or chicken.

asian-flavoured mayos

BELOW: To make chilli-coriander mayonnaise, combine 1 cup (300g) store-bought whole-egg mayonnaise with a pinch of chilli flakes and ¼ cup chopped coriander (cilantro) leaves. Serve with chicken, seafood, steamed vegetables and salads. To make wasabi mayonnaise, combine 1 cup (300g) store-bought whole-egg mayonnaise with 1 tablespoon wasabi paste. Serve mayos with seafood and Asian salads.

These pungently flavoured mayonnaises and piquant salsas are the culinary equivalent of a warm-up. They're bound to kick-start a bland or subtly flavoured dish into a bolder dimension.

aïoli & lemon mayo

ABOVE: To make the aïoli place 1 cup (300g) store-bought whole-egg mayonnaise in a bowl with 2–3 cloves crushed garlic and stir to combine. Serve with grilled meats and vegetables, or as an accompaniment to seafood. To make the lemon mayo, place 1 cup (300g) store-bought whole-egg mayonnaise in a bowl and stir in 2 tablespoons lemon juice. Serve mayos with chicken, seafood and steamed vegetables.

green mango lime salsa

LEFT: Combine 1 peeled and finely sliced green mango, 2 tablespoons lime juice, 1 teaspoon caster (superfine) sugar, 1 teaspoon fish sauce, 1 thinly sliced long red chilli, 1 teaspoon thinly sliced ginger and 1 cup coriander (cilantro) leaves in a small bowl and toss gently to combine. Serve salsa with soy-basted or Asian-flavoured grilled or pan-fried beef, chicken, pork, fish and shellfish.

squashed cherry tomato salsa

RIGHT: Squash 250g cherry tomatoes to remove seeds, place in a bowl with 1 tablespoon finely grated lemon rind, ¼ cup oregano leaves, ⅓ cup finely chopped green onions (scallions), 2 tablespoons olive oil, 1 tablespoon malt vinegar and 1 teaspoon caster (superfine) sugar and toss to combine. Serve salsa with pasta, or as an accompaniment to grilled meat, chicken and seafood.

cucumber salsa

BELOW: Place ½ cup (125ml) white wine vinegar and 1 tablespoon caster (superfine) sugar in a small saucepan over high heat, bring to the boil and cook for 2–3 minutes. Place 4 sliced and seeded Lebanese cucumbers and 1 cup mint leaves in a bowl, pour the hot vinegar mixture over and stir to combine. Serve salsa cold or at room temperature with grilled fish, lamb or chicken and store-bought hummus or as a cooling accompaniment to curries with heat.

Transform a simple steak, char-grilled chicken, fish or vegies into something special with the addition of a flavour-packed salsa. Marry prime produce with herbs, capers or olives for a fresh take on tasty.

salsa verde

ABOVE: Combine ½ cup flatleaf parsley leaves, ½ cup mint leaves, ¼ cup dill leaves, 1 teaspoon of Dijon mustard, 1 tablespoon rinsed salted capers, 1 tablespoon finely grated lemon rind and 2 tablespoons olive oil in the bowl of a small food processor and process until coarsely chopped. Serve salsa as a sauce for pasta or with veal, chicken or grilled seafood.

olive & pine nut salsa

LEFT: Place ½ cup (60g) pitted black olives, ½ cup flatleaf parsley leaves, ½ cup finely chopped basil leaves, 1 tablespoon lemon zest, ¼ cup (60ml) olive oil, ½ cup toasted pine nuts and sea salt in a bowl and stir to combine. Serve salsa with grilled, barbecued or roasted beef, chicken, lamb or seafood or with pasta and couscous.

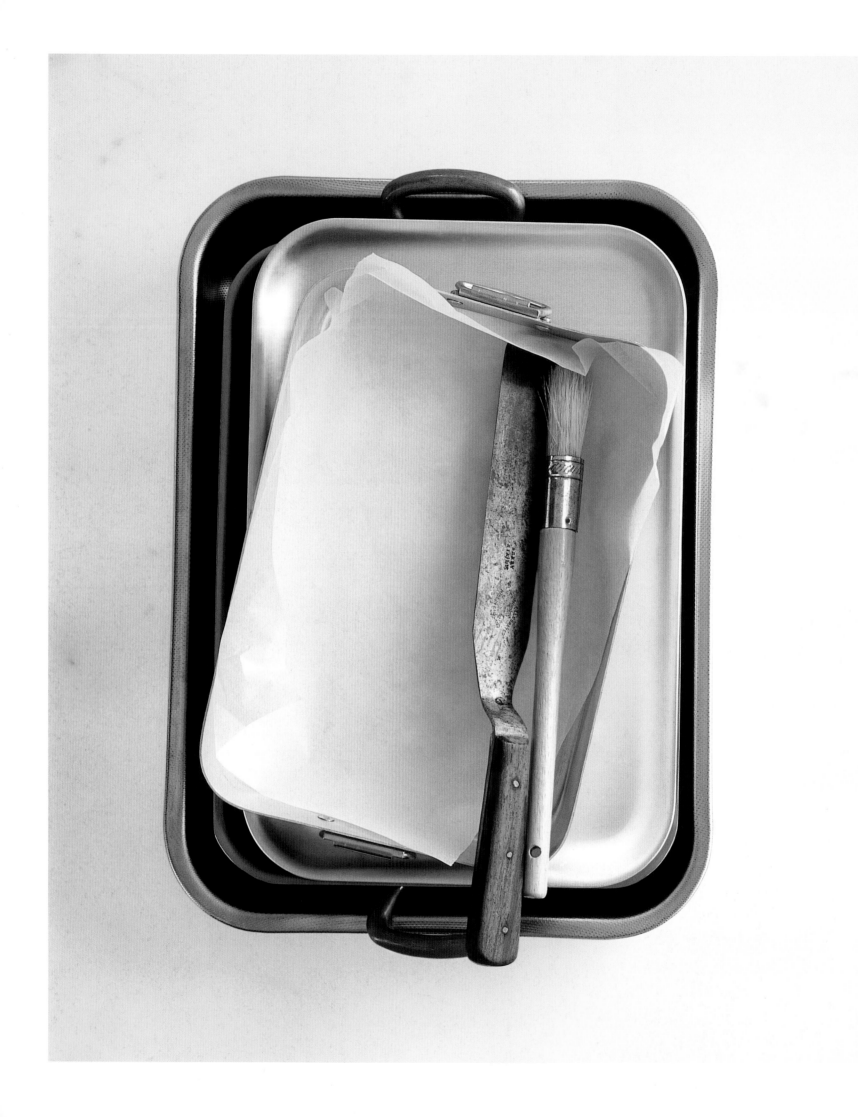

ONE DISH

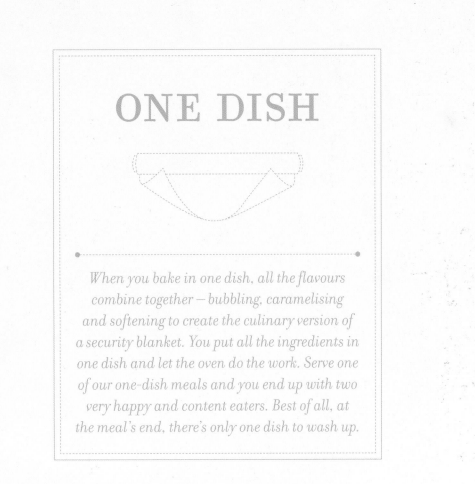

When you bake in one dish, all the flavours combine together — bubbling, caramelising and softening to create the culinary version of a security blanket. You put all the ingredients in one dish and let the oven do the work. Serve one of our one-dish meals and you end up with two very happy and content eaters. Best of all, at the meal's end, there's only one dish to wash up.

ONION MARMALADE TART

LEMON-FETA CHICKEN

onion marmalade tart

1 sheet (25cm x 25cm) store-bought puff pastry, thawed
¾ cup (160g) store-bought onion marmalade
or caramelised onions
8 pitted olives
8 anchovies, optional
2 teaspoons thyme sprigs
cracked black pepper
shaved parmesan, to serve
rocket (arugula) leaves, to serve

Preheat oven to 180°C (355°F). Trim edges of pastry and place on a sheet of non-stick baking paper on a baking tray. Spoon the onion marmalade onto pastry and top with olives, anchovies and thyme. Bake for 20–25 minutes or until pastry is puffed and golden. Sprinkle with pepper and serve with parmesan and rocket. **SERVES 2.**

Frozen puff and shortcrust pastries are among the cook's greatest stand-bys. Choose varieties made with butter for their superior flavour. To achieve that over-the-top flaky crown on the top of your pie you will probably need to layer two sheets of store-bought ready-rolled puff pastry.

lemon-feta chicken

2 x 200g chicken breast fillets, trimmed
200g feta, thickly sliced
5 sprigs oregano
1 tablespoon lemon zest
2 tablespoons lemon juice
olive oil, for sprinkling
cracked black pepper
green salad, optional

Preheat oven to 180°C (355°F). Place chicken, feta, oregano, lemon zest and juice in a baking dish. Sprinkle with olive oil and pepper. Bake for 18 minutes, or until chicken is cooked through. Serve with a simple green salad, if desired. **SERVES 2.**

baked three-cheese risotto

1 cup (200g) arborio or other risotto rice
2½ cups (625ml) chicken or vegetable stock
1 leek, very finely chopped
1 teaspoon chopped oregano leaves
30g butter
⅓ cup (25g) finely grated parmesan
sea salt and cracked black pepper
150g creamy blue cheese, sliced
150g fresh ricotta
4 slices prosciutto
extra finely grated parmesan, to serve

Preheat oven to 190°C (375°F). Place rice, stock, leek, oregano and butter in a baking dish and cover tightly with a lid or a piece of aluminium foil. Bake for 40 minutes or until the rice is soft. Stir in parmesan, salt and pepper and continue stirring for 5 minutes or until risotto is creamy and remaining stock has been absorbed. Divide risotto between serving plates and top with blue cheese, ricotta, prosciutto and extra parmesan to serve. **SERVES 2.**

BAKED THREE-CHEESE RISOTTO

baked ricotta & pumpkin salad

400g piece fresh ricotta
1 tablespoon olive oil
½ teaspoon sweet paprika
1 tablespoon oregano leaves
sea salt and cracked black pepper
1 tablespoon finely grated parmesan
500g pumpkin, peeled and halved
extra olive oil, for drizzling
200g cherry tomatoes
rocket (arugula) leaves, to serve
½ cup (75g) pitted Kalamata olives, to serve

Preheat oven to 180°C (355°F). Place ricotta at one end of a baking dish lined with non-stick baking paper. Combine olive oil, paprika, oregano, salt and pepper and spoon over the ricotta. Sprinkle with parmesan. Place pumpkin at the other end of the baking dish and drizzle with a little extra oil. Bake for 25 minutes, add tomatoes, drizzle with some more oil and bake for a further 25 minutes or until ricotta is golden and pumpkin is soft. Serve with rocket and olives. **SERVES 2.**

soy & ginger baked fish

¼ cup (60ml) soy sauce
1 tablespoon grated ginger
4 green onions (scallions), sliced
1 teaspoon sesame oil
1 teaspoon brown sugar
400g fillet firm-fleshed white fish
200g gai larn (Chinese broccoli), trimmed
½ cup coriander (cilantro) leaves
½ cup basil leaves
1 long red chilli, chopped (optional)

Preheat oven to 180°C (355°F). Place soy, ginger, onion, sesame oil and sugar into a shallow dish. Add the fish and marinate for 5 minutes each side. Place the gai larn into a baking dish lined with non-stick baking paper and top with the fish and marinade. Cover with aluminium foil and bake for 15 minutes or until fish is tender. To serve top with coriander, basil and chopped chilli, if desired. **SERVES 2.**

herb & mozzarella wrapped veal

2 tomatoes, each cut into 4 slices
olive oil, for drizzling
1 tablespoon oregano leaves
sea salt and cracked black pepper
4 large slices pancetta
4 x 60g thin veal steaks
2 teaspoons thyme leaves
2 teaspoons oregano leaves, extra
4 slices mozzarella
rocket (arugula) leaves, to serve

Place tomato in a baking tray. Drizzle with olive oil, oregano, salt and pepper. Place pancetta on a board and top with a piece of veal. Sprinkle with thyme and extra oregano and place a slice of mozzarella on one end so you can fold the pancetta and veal over to enclose the cheese. Place veal beside the tomato, drizzle with olive oil and cook under a preheated grill for 5–7 minutes or until veal is cooked and pancetta is crispy. Divide veal and tomato between plates, serve with rocket. **SERVES 2**.

roast tomato chicken

2 x 220g tomatoes, halved
8 sprigs thyme
16 basil leaves
8 pitted Kalamata olives
2 x 200g chicken breast fillets, cut into thirds
1 tablespoon thyme leaves, extra
2/3 cup (50g) finely grated parmesan
sea salt and cracked black pepper
olive oil, for drizzling
rocket (arugula) leaves, to serve

Place tomatoes cut side up in a baking tray lined with non-stick baking paper. Make a few slits in the tops of the tomatoes with a knife. Stuff the slits with thyme, basil and olives. Sprinkle both sides of chicken with extra thyme, parmesan, salt and pepper. Add chicken to the baking tray, drizzle with oil and place under a preheated hot grill for 6–8 minutes, or until chicken is cooked through. Divide rocket between serving plates and top with the chicken and tomatoes. Spoon over pan juices to serve. **SERVES 2**.

CRUNCHY PARMESAN–CRUMBED CHICKEN

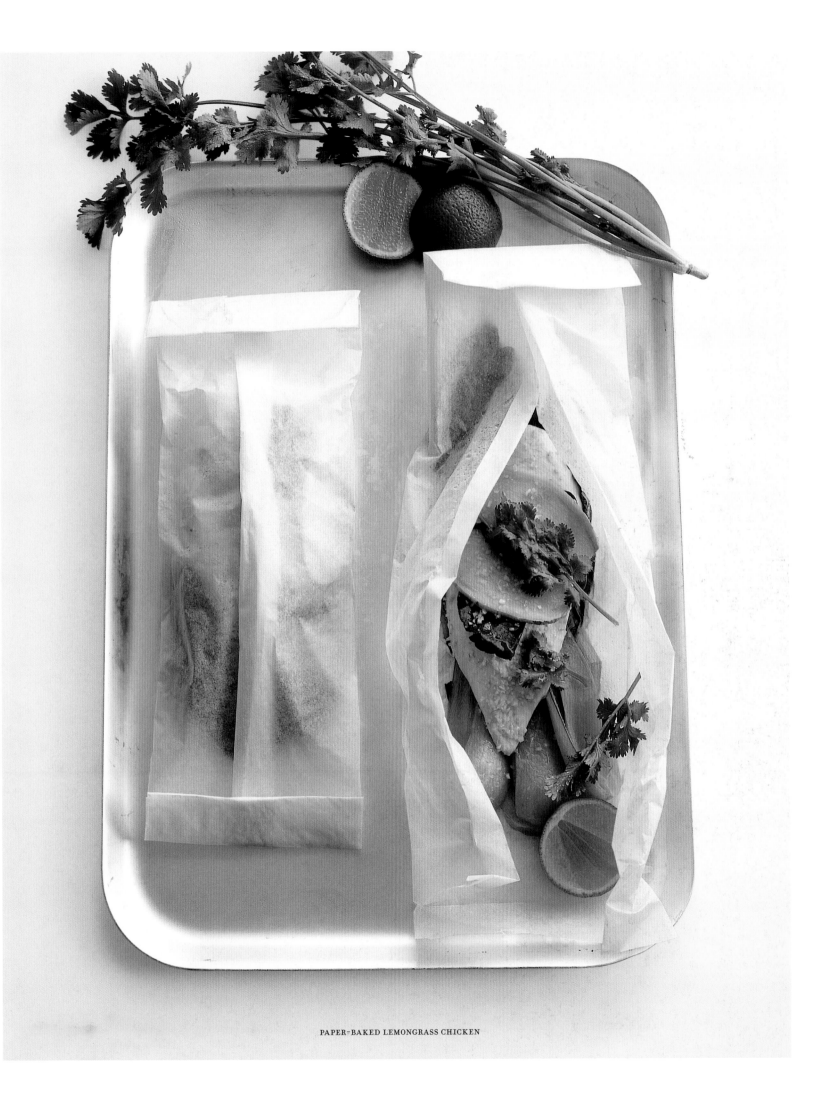

PAPER-BAKED LEMONGRASS CHICKEN

crunchy parmesan-crumbed chicken

1 cup (70g) fresh breadcrumbs
¼ cup (20g) finely grated parmesan
30g butter, melted
1 tablespoon finely chopped thyme leaves
cracked black pepper
2 x 200g chicken breast fillets, trimmed and halved
lemon wedges and green salad, to serve

Preheat oven to 200°C (390°F). Combine the breadcrumbs, parmesan, butter, thyme and pepper. Place the chicken into a baking dish lined with non-stick baking paper. Top chicken with breadcrumb mixture. Bake for 10 minutes or until the chicken is cooked through and the crumbs are golden. Serve with lemon wedges and green salad. SERVES 2.

If you're going to the trouble of dragging the food processor or blender out of the cupboard to make fresh breadcrumbs, you might as well make a heap and freeze them for future use. Freeze the portions in zip-lock plastic bags so you'll always have breadcrumbs handy for making stuffings and crunchy toppings.

paper-baked lemongrass chicken

2 baby bok choy, halved
2 x 200g chicken breast fillets, trimmed
sesame oil, for sprinkling
1 stalk lemongrass, trimmed and finely chopped
4 kaffir lime leaves, bruised
4 slices ginger, cut into matchsticks
¼ cup coriander (cilantro) leaves
1 lime, halved, to serve

Preheat oven to 180°C (355°F). Cut 2 large pieces of baking paper. In the middle of each piece of paper place 2 pieces of bok choy topped with a chicken fillet. Sprinkle with sesame oil, lemongrass, lime leaves and ginger. Fold the edges of the paper together to seal. Place chicken parcels on a baking tray and bake for 12 minutes. Carefully unfold the paper. Top with coriander and serve with lime halves. SERVES 2.

pan-roasted shellfish

4 green (raw) scampi, halved and cleaned
6 green (raw) prawns (shrimp), heads removed and halved
4 soft-shell crabs, halved
6 scallops on the half shell
80g butter, softened
1 tablespoon salted capers, rinsed and chopped
2 cloves garlic, crushed
1 teaspoon chilli flakes
1 teaspoon grated lemon rind
1 tablespoon lemon thyme leaves
cracked black pepper
lemon halves, to serve

Preheat oven to 200°C (390°F). Arrange scampi, prawns, crab and scallops in a baking dish lined with non-stick baking paper. Mix together butter, capers, garlic, chilli, lemon rind, lemon thyme and pepper. Spread butter over the shellfish. Bake the seafood for 10 minutes or until cooked through and serve with lemon. SERVES 2.

PAN-ROASTED SHELLFISH

vine-leaf roast chicken

750g potatoes, peeled and thinly sliced
1 onion, sliced
sea salt and cracked black pepper
1 tablespoon olive oil
2 tablespoons pine nuts, chopped
1 teaspoon grated lemon rind
1 tablespoon finely chopped flatleaf parsley leaves
1 teaspoon olive oil, extra
2 x 200g chicken breast fillets
2 large vine leaves in brine, rinsed
extra olive oil, for brushing

Preheat oven to 200°C (390°F). Line a baking dish with non-stick baking paper. Toss together the potato, onion, salt, pepper and oil and place in the baking dish. Bake for 20 minutes. Combine pine nuts, lemon rind, parsley and extra oil. Spread mixture on top of chicken and wrap each piece of chicken in a vine leaf. Brush with the extra oil and place on top of potatoes. Bake for 20 minutes or until chicken is cooked through and the potatoes are tender. **SERVES 2.**

baked pumpkin & pancetta risotto

1 cup (200g) arborio or other risotto rice
2½ cups (625ml) chicken or vegetable stock
30g butter
1 tablespoon small sage leaves
400g pumpkin, peeled and diced
6 thin slices pancetta, coarsely chopped
⅓ cup (25g) finely grated parmesan
sea salt and cracked black pepper
extra grated parmesan, to serve

Preheat oven to 190°C (375°F). Combine rice, stock, butter, sage, pumpkin and pancetta in a baking dish and cover tightly with a lid or aluminium foil. Bake for 45 minutes or until the rice is soft. Stir in parmesan, salt and pepper and continue stirring for 5 minutes or until the risotto is creamy and remaining stock is absorbed. Divide risotto between plates and top with extra parmesan to serve. **SERVES 2.**

molten mozzarella in prosciutto

4 slices sourdough bread
2 tablespoons olive oil
1 clove garlic, crushed
12 basil leaves
3 ripe tomatoes, thickly sliced
1 tablespoon balsamic vinegar
sea salt and cracked black pepper
2 large fresh buffalo mozzarella, halved
4 large thin slices prosciutto

Preheat oven to 200°C (390°F). Place bread in a baking dish. Combine the oil and garlic and brush over the bread. Top bread with basil and tomato. Sprinkle with vinegar, salt and pepper and bake for 15 minutes or until the tomato is soft. Wrap each piece of mozzarella in a slice of prosciutto and place on top of the tomato. Bake for a further 10–15 minutes or until mozzarella is melted and prosciutto is crisp. **SERVES 2.**

chicken pot pies

200g cooked chicken, chopped
¼ cup (60g) sour cream
75g grated cheddar
2 tablespoons chopped chives
sea salt and cracked black pepper
1 sheet (25cm x 25cm) store-bought puff pastry, thawed
1 egg, lightly beaten

Preheat oven to 180°C (355°F). Combine chicken, sour cream, cheese, chives, salt and pepper. Cut 2 x 11cm rounds from the pastry. Divide the chicken mixture between 2 x 1-cup (250ml) capacity ramekins and top with pastry rounds. Brush pastry with egg and bake for 20 minutes or until the pastry is puffed and golden brown. **SERVES 2.**

MOROCCAN-SPICED BAKED LAMB

ROASTED VEGETABLE & PESTO SALAD

moroccan-spiced baked lamb

1 tablespoon olive oil
1 tablespoon chopped preserved lemon rind (G)
1 tablespoon lemon juice
2 cloves garlic, crushed
¼ cup coarsely chopped coriander (cilantro) leaves
2 teaspoons ground coriander (cilantro) seeds
1 teaspoon smoked paprika
sea salt and cracked black pepper
400g lamb rump roast
6 chat (baby) potatoes, halved
3 carrots, peeled and halved
7 cloves garlic, extra, unpeeled
1 tablespoon olive oil, extra

Place oil, lemon rind, juice, garlic, coriander leaves and seeds, paprika, salt and pepper in a food processor and process until mixture forms a paste. Preheat oven to 180°C (355°F). Spread paste thickly over the lamb and allow to marinate for 20 minutes. While the lamb is marinating, place potatoes, carrots, extra garlic, extra oil and salt into a baking dish and bake for 20 minutes. Add the lamb to the baking dish and bake for 30–35 minutes or until cooked to your liking. To serve divide potatoes, carrots and garlic between plates. Slice lamb into thick slices and serve with the roasted vegetables. **SERVES 2.**

We just adore the exotic sweet flavour and extra depth that a pinch of smoked paprika lends all sorts of savoury dishes. Made from dried capsicum, with intense colour ranging from bright orange to blood-red, it's worth searching out a good Spanish variety. Remember, however, that a little bit goes a long way so use sparingly at first.

roasted vegetable & pesto salad

200g parsnip, peeled and quartered
300g orange sweet potato (kumara), peeled and quartered
200g fennel, quartered
400g potatoes, peeled and quartered
1 tablespoon olive oil
8 sprigs thyme
sea salt and cracked black pepper
250g cherry tomatoes
120g green olives
baby spinach leaves, to serve
pesto dressing
2 tablespoons chopped mint leaves
2 tablespoons chopped basil leaves
¼ cup (20g) finely grated parmesan
2 tablespoons olive oil

To make pesto dressing, place mint, basil, parmesan and oil in a small bowl and stir to combine. Preheat oven to 200°C (390°F). Place parsnip, sweet potato, fennel and potato in a baking dish, add oil, thyme, salt and pepper and toss to coat evenly. Bake for 20 minutes, then add tomatoes and olives and bake for a further 20 minutes. Divide roasted vegetables between plates and serve with spinach and pesto dressing. **SERVES 2.**

baked garlic mussels & couscous

3 cloves garlic, crushed
1 tablespoon grated ginger
¾ cup (180ml) boiling water
¾ cup (150g) instant couscous
30g butter melted
1kg mussels, scrubbed
½ cup coriander (cilantro) leaves
lime wedges, to serve

Preheat oven to 180°C (355°F). Combine garlic, ginger and the boiling water and pour over couscous in the bottom of a baking dish. Drizzle with butter and top couscous with mussels. Cover dish tightly with a lid or aluminium foil and bake for 20 minutes or until mussels have opened. Sprinkle with coriander and serve with lime wedges. **SERVES 2.**

BAKED GARLIC MUSSELS & COUSCOUS

marinated vegetable tart

1 sheet (25cm x 25cm) store-bought puff pastry, thawed
300g store-bought marinated vegetables,⁺ drained
2 teaspoons oregano leaves
110g feta or soft goat's cheese, roughly chopped
olive oil, for drizzling

Preheat oven to 180°C (355°F). Cut pastry in half and place pieces side by side on a baking tray lined with non-stick baking paper. Top the pastries with vegetables, oregano and cheese. Drizzle with olive oil and bake for 18–20 minutes or until pastry is puffed and golden. Serve warm or cold. SERVES 2.

⁺Marinated vegetable mix might contain eggplant, capsicum, semi-dried tomatoes, mushrooms, zucchini and artichoke hearts.

herb & garlic roast chicken

1 small chicken, cut into pieces
60g soft butter
2 tablespoons chopped flatleaf parsley leaves
2 tablespoons lemon thyme leaves
sea salt and cracked black pepper
8 cloves garlic, unpeeled
steamed green vegetables, to serve

Preheat oven to 200°C (390°F). Place chicken pieces in a baking dish lined with non-stick baking paper. Combine butter, parsley, thyme, salt and pepper and rub over the chicken. Add garlic to the tray and bake for 30 minutes or until the chicken is browned and cooked through. Serve with steamed greens. SERVES 2.

crushed zucchini pie

10 sheets filo pastry
melted butter, for brushing
2 zucchini (courgette), grated
4 eggs, lightly beaten
¾ cup (180ml) cream
½ cup (60g) grated cheddar
sea salt and cracked black pepper

Preheat oven to 180°C (355°F). Brush 2 sheets of pastry with butter and fold the pastry to fit the base and sides of a shallow 1¾-cup (430ml) capacity ovenproof pie dish. Repeat with the other pie dish. Combine zucchini, eggs, cream, cheese, salt and pepper and pour into the pie dishes. Brush the remaining sheets of pastry with butter. Fold each pastry sheet in half and scrunch. Pile the pastry on top of the pies. Bake for 35–40 minutes or until filling is set and pastry is golden. **SERVES 2**.

baked fish & chips

1kg potatoes, sliced into chips
2 lemons, quartered
1 tablespoon olive oil
1 tablespoon lemon thyme leaves
sea salt and cracked black pepper
2 x 180g firm-fleshed white fish fillets
20g butter, melted
2 cloves garlic, sliced
1 teaspoon lemon thyme leaves, extra

Preheat oven to 200°C (390°F). Toss potatoes and lemon with oil, thyme, salt and pepper and place in a baking dish. Bake for 45 minutes, turning once, or until golden and crisp. Move the potatoes to the side and add fish to the dish. Brush with the combined butter, garlic and extra lemon thyme. Bake for a further 10 minutes or until fish is cooked through. **SERVES 2**.

BAKED HALOUMI & SOURDOUGH SALAD

QUINCE-ROASTED LAMB

baked haloumi & sourdough salad

4 thick slices sourdough bread, torn into chunks
8 cloves garlic, unpeeled
250g haloumi, torn into chunks
200g grape tomatoes, pricked with a knife
2 tablespoons olive oil
pinch chilli flakes
½ cup flatleaf parsley leaves
½ cup mint leaves
1 tablespoon lemon juice
1 tablespoon olive oil

Preheat oven to 180°C (355°F). Toss bread, garlic, haloumi and tomatoes together in a baking dish. Combine oil and chilli and drizzle over the bread mixture. Bake for 20 minutes, toss bread mixture then continue cooking for another 10 minutes. Remove from oven and place bread mixture in a bowl. Add parsley, mint, lemon juice and olive oil and toss to combine. SERVES 2.

Haloumi is a firm white Cypriot cheese made from sheep's milk. It has a stringy texture and holds its shape during grilling and pan-frying so is great to use for kebabs and salads. If you have trouble locating it in the shops, you could use a firm feta as a substitute.

quince-roasted lamb

4 carrots, peeled and quartered
3 rosemary sprigs
2 tablespoons brown sugar
sea salt
2 x 200g lamb backstraps (boneless loins)
¼ cup (75g) quince paste
12 slices pancetta

Preheat oven to 200°C (390°F). Place carrots, rosemary, sugar and salt in a baking dish lined with non-stick baking paper and toss to coat. Bake for 45 minutes. Spread lamb with quince paste. Arrange 6 slices of pancetta on a board, slightly overlapping. Place a piece of lamb on pancetta and fold to enclose. Repeat with remaining pancetta and lamb loin. Place lamb on top of carrots and bake for 12–15 minutes for medium or until cooked to your liking. Slice lamb thickly and serve with carrots. SERVES 2.

melted mozzarella chicken

250g cherry tomatoes, halved
½ cup (75g) pitted Kalamata olives
1 tablespoon olive oil
4 thick slices mozzarella
8 basil leaves
2 x 200g chicken breast fillets, halved lengthways
8 slices pancetta
green salad, optional

Preheat oven to 200°C (390°F). Place cherry tomatoes, olives and olive oil in a baking dish and bake for 10 minutes or until tomatoes are soft. Place a slice of mozzarella and 2 basil leaves on each piece of chicken and wrap with 2 slices of pancetta to enclose. Place the wrapped chicken on top of the tomato mixture and bake for a further 12–15 minutes or until chicken is cooked through. Serve with a green salad, if desired. SERVES 2.

MELTED MOZZARELLA CHICKEN

CHEATS 5.

vegetable sides

Just as accessories can make or break
an outfit, the right vegie accompaniments
can elevate a simple meal into a special
occasion. We've tweaked some traditional
favourites and come up with some fresh new
flavour combinations that are bound to have
your family and friends looking at common
or garden vegies in a whole new light.

porcini mash

RIGHT: Peel and coarsely chop 1.2kg potatoes. Add to a saucepan with 2 tablespoons coarsely chopped dried porcini mushrooms, cover with salted water and place over high heat. Bring to the boil and cook for 15 minutes, or until the potatoes are tender. Drain and mash potatoes and porcini with 80g butter, ½ cup (125ml) milk, sea salt and cracked black pepper until smooth and creamy. Serve the porcini mash with grilled or roasted meats, chicken dishes and slow-cooked braises. **SERVES 4.**

simple potato cake

BELOW: Peel and chop 1kg potatoes. Place potatoes in a frying pan with an ovenproof handle and cover with water. Simmer for 8 minutes or until soft. Drain well and return to pan. Add 1 tablespoon olive oil, 30g butter, 1 teaspoon chopped rosemary leaves, sea salt and cracked black pepper. Toss potatoes and mash lightly till the potatoes stick together. Bake in a preheated 200°C (390°F) oven for 30 minutes or until the potatoes are crisp and golden. Cut into large wedges to serve. **SERVES 4.**

The not-so-humble spud dresses for dinner in an array of different guises that range from elegantly creamy mashes and crackling crisp rösti to a stylishly simple potato cake.

parsnip & rosemary rösti

ABOVE: Peel 600g potatoes and 250g parsnips, grate coarsely and combine with 60g melted butter, 2 teaspoons chopped rosemary leaves, sea salt flakes and cracked black pepper. Divide mixture into 8 and place on a baking tray lined with non-stick baking paper. Flatten the mixture and bake in a preheated 180°C (355°F) oven for 35 minutes or until the rösti are golden and crisp. Serve as an accompaniment to grilled and roasted meats, chicken, vegetables or seafood. **SERVES 4.**

white bean & rosemary mash

LEFT: Peel and boil 1kg potatoes until tender, drain and return to the pan over low heat. Add 60g butter, 2 tablespoons milk, 1 teaspoon chopped rosemary leaves and sea salt and mash until smooth. Add a 400g can drained and rinsed white (cannellini) or butter beans and mash until the beans are lightly broken through the mash. Serve with an extra wedge of butter. Mash is best with grilled or roasted meats, chicken, vegetables or fish and dishes with plenty of sauce to be soaked up. **SERVES 4.**

spiced sweet potato

RIGHT: Peel and cut 4 orange sweet potatoes (kumara) into wedges. Combine ⅓ cup (80ml) olive oil with 1 teaspoon smoked paprika, 1 teaspoon ground coriander and 1 teaspoon brown sugar. Place the sweet potato into a baking dish, brush with the paprika oil and sprinkle with sea salt and cracked black pepper. Bake in a preheated 200°C (390°F) oven for 25 minutes or until the sweet potato is tender. Serve with roasted meats or seafood. **SERVES 4.**

lime & chilli corn

BELOW: Place 50g butter, 1 teaspoon finely grated lime rind, a pinch of chilli flakes, 2 teaspoons chopped coriander (cilantro), sea salt and cracked black pepper into a saucepan and cook until bubbling. Brush the butter mixture over 4 cooked corn cobs and serve with remaining butter on the side. Serve with grilled or roasted meats, chicken, vegetables or seafood. Also a great side dish as part of a barbecue menu. **SERVES 4.**

Vegetables move from support act to centre stage when teamed with boldly flavoured herbs and spices. Joosh up even the most basic grills or roasts with these strong statements.

baked polenta chips

ABOVE: Heat 3 cups (750ml) chicken stock and 1½ cups (375ml) water in a saucepan until boiling. Slowly add 1½ cups (255g) instant polenta and cook, stirring, until soft. Stir in ½ cup (40g) finely grated parmesan. Pour into a baking tray lined with non-stick baking paper and allow to set. Turn out and cut into chunky chips. Brush chips with melted butter and bake, turning once, in a preheated 200°C (390°F) oven for 35 minutes or until the polenta chips are golden and crisp. **SERVES 4.**

maple roast pumpkin

LEFT: Melt 30g butter in a medium non-stick frying pan over medium heat, add 6 slices peeled pumpkin and cook 2 minutes each side. Add 50g extra butter, ¼ cup (60ml) maple syrup, sea salt and cracked black pepper and cover pan with a lid of non-stick baking paper cut to fit the pan's circumference. Simmer for 10–12 minutes or until the pumpkin is tender. Remove paper from pan, add ¼ cup (60ml) water and simmer for a further 1–2 minutes or until maple mixture forms a thin sauce. **SERVES 4.**

onion & garlic butter beans

RIGHT: Combine 40g butter and 1 tablespoon olive oil and cook over medium-high heat in a non-stick frying pan. Add 2 sliced onions and cook for 5 minutes or until golden. Add 4 cloves sliced garlic and cook for 1 minute. Add a 400g can drained and rinsed white (cannellini) or butter beans and cook for 4 minutes or until beans are heated through. Stir through 150g baby spinach leaves, salt and pepper and sprinkle with grated parmesan. Serve with grilled or roasted meats, chicken or fish. **SERVES 4.**

spinach with mozzarella

BELOW: Remove leaves from 3 bunches English spinach. Melt 30g butter in a large non-stick frying pan over medium heat. Add 2 cloves crushed garlic and 1 teaspoon finely grated lemon rind and cook for 1 minute. Add the spinach and toss until leaves are wilted. Divide among 4 buttered ramekins. Make a small hole in the middle of the spinach and place a 30g piece of mozzarella in each hole. Bake in a preheated 180°C (355°F) oven for 10 minutes or until the mozzarella is melted and brown. **SERVES 4.**

There's no need to say "eat your greens" when they provide texture and flavour contrast as well as a surprise element on the plate. With this selection it's more than likely your guests will want seconds.

ginger & chilli snake beans

ABOVE: Heat a deep frying pan or wok over medium-high heat. Add 2 teaspoons sesame oil, 1 tablespoon grated ginger, 2 finely sliced long red chillies, 2 sliced cloves garlic and cook for 1 minute. Add 400g trimmed and halved snake or green beans, ¼ cup (60ml) chicken or vegetable stock and 1 teaspoon soy sauce and cook, stirring, for 4–5 minutes or until the beans are tender. Serve with grilled or roasted meats, chicken, vegetables or fish and Asian-inspired curries and stir-fries. **SERVES 4.**

lemon & garlic roast broccoli or cauliflower

LEFT: Preheat oven to 180°C (355°F). Place 1kg broccoli or cauliflower florets, 1 lemon cut into wedges, 2 tablespoons of olive oil, 8 unpeeled cloves garlic, 8 peeled eschalots, sea salt flakes and cracked black pepper into a large baking dish and toss to combine. Bake the vegetables for 40 minutes or until they are browned and tender. Serve with grilled or roasted meats, chicken, seafood or, as the base to a salad. **SERVES 4.**

SOME NOW
SOME LATER

I'd always thought of freezing meals as a vaguely old-fashioned concept best left (with the crock pot and fondue set) to my mother's generation. But now that I too am a working parent, the prospect of a night off thanks to a dinner that's ready to be reheated has great appeal. We've reinvented 'make and freeze' with fresh, flavour-packed recipes everyone will love.

BEEF & BEER INDIVIDUAL PIES

BROCCOLI & BACON SOUP

beef & beer individual pies

2 tablespoons olive oil
1kg chuck steak, cubed
2 brown onions, chopped
2 cloves garlic, crushed
4 sprigs thyme
2 bay leaves
1½ cups (375ml) beer
2 cups (500ml) beef stock
8 chat (baby) potatoes, quartered
2 tablespoons cornflour
2 tablespoons water
1 cup (120g) fresh or frozen peas
2 sheets (25cm x 25cm) store-bought shortcrust pastry
beaten egg, for brushing

Heat oil in a saucepan over medium–high heat. Add beef and cook, in batches, until well browned. Remove beef using a slotted spoon and set aside. Add onion, garlic, thyme and bay leaves and cook for 3 minutes or until onion is soft. Add beer and cook for 2 minutes to reduce slightly. Return beef to the pan and add stock and potatoes. Cover pan, reduce heat and simmer gently for 1 hour, or until beef is tender. Combine cornflour and water, stir into the beef mixture for 3 minutes or until sauce thickens. Remove from heat, add peas and cool the mixture slightly before dividing among 6 x 1⅓-cup (330ml) capacity ramekins or pie dishes. Preheat the oven to 200°C (390°F). Cut pastry lids to fit ramekins, place on top of pies and brush with egg. Bake pies for 20 minutes or until pastry is light golden. To freeze, wrap the pie dishes in layers of baking paper, plastic wrap and aluminium foil to seal. Freeze for up to 3 months. SERVES 2 NOW & 4 LATER.

The best dishes for freezing have a high liquid content, which keeps the ingredients juicy and packed with flavour even after reheating. For this reason pies and baked pasta dishes are natural freezer candidates, as of course are slow-cooked braises, curries and soups.

broccoli & bacon soup

1 onion, chopped
4 rashers bacon, rind removed, chopped
400g potatoes, peeled and diced
1 litre chicken stock
400g broccoli, chopped
2 tablespoons chopped mint
sea salt and cracked black pepper

Place onion and bacon in a large saucepan over medium–high heat. Cook for 5 minutes or until well browned. Remove onion and bacon from saucepan and set aside. Put potato and stock in the pan, bring to the boil, add broccoli and cook for 8 minutes or until broccoli and potatoes are soft. Place soup in a blender or use a stick mixer to blend until smooth. Add onion and bacon, mint, salt and pepper and stir to combine. Ladle into bowls to serve. To freeze, place in an airtight container, seal and freeze for up to three months. SERVES 2 NOW & 2 LATER.

pumpkin, ricotta & basil lasagne

1.2kg fresh ricotta cheese
2 cups (160g) grated parmesan
⅓ cup chopped chives
½ cup shredded basil
1 tablespoon finely grated lemon rind
sea salt and cracked black pepper
¼ cup coarsely chopped oregano leaves
1.25 litres tomato passata (G)
600g lasagne sheets
1.5kg peeled and seeded pumpkin, thinly sliced
1 cup (100g) grated mozzarella

Preheat oven to 180°C (355°F). Combine ricotta, half the grated parmesan, chives, basil, lemon rind, salt and pepper in a bowl and mix well. Stir oregano into passata. Place a layer of lasagne sheets into the base of a greased 20cm x 35cm baking dish. Top with a third of the pumpkin and spoon over a third of the passata mixture. Top with a third of the ricotta mixture and another layer of lasagne sheets. Repeat layers, ending with a layer of lasagne sheets and the remaining ricotta mixture. Sprinkle with mozzarella and the remaining parmesan, cover with aluminium foil and bake 1½ hours. Remove foil and bake for a further 15 minutes or until the cheese is golden brown and the lasagne is cooked through. Freeze remaining portions for up to 3 months. SERVES 2 NOW & 6 LATER.

PUMPKIN, RICOTTA & BASIL LASAGNE

spinach, ricotta & dill pies

4 sheets (25cm x 25cm) store-bought shortcrust pastry, thawed
spinach-ricotta filling
250g frozen spinach, thawed
600g ricotta
3 eggs
½ cup (40g) finely grated parmesan
2 green onions (scallions), finely sliced
2 tablespoons coarsely chopped flatleaf parsley leaves
2 tablespoons coarsely chopped dill leaves
sea salt and cracked black pepper

Preheat oven to 180°C (355°F). Cut pastry to fit 4 x 1-cup (250ml) pie dishes, allowing for an overhang. To make the spinch–ricotta filling, squeeze out excess water from spinach, place in bowl with ricotta, eggs, parmesan, onion, parsley, dill, salt and pepper and mix together well. Divide filling between pastry-lined dishes and bake for 30 minutes or until filling sets. To freeze, wrap pie dishes in a layer of baking paper, then plastic wrap and aluminium foil to seal. Freeze for up to 3 months. **SERVES 2 NOW & 2 LATER**.

coriander chicken curry

1 onion, chopped
1 tablespoon grated ginger
2 cloves garlic, chopped
1 cup coriander (cilantro) leaves and 3 cleaned roots
2 teaspoons fish sauce
4 kaffir lime leaves
4 coarsely chopped long green chillies
2 tablespoons vegetable oil
8 x 140g chicken thigh fillets, cut into thirds
½ cup (125ml) chicken stock
1 cup (250ml) coconut milk
200g beans, trimmed and halved

Combine onion, ginger, garlic, coriander leaves and roots, fish sauce, lime leaves and chilli in a blender or small food processor and process to a coarse paste. Heat vegetable oil in a non-stick frying pan over medium heat, add curry paste and cook, stirring occasionally, for 5 minutes. Add chicken and stir to coat in paste. Add stock and coconut milk and bring to the boil. Reduce heat and simmer, uncovered, for 20 minutes. Add beans and simmer for a further 5 minutes. Freeze for up to 3 months. **SERVES 2 NOW & 2 LATER**.

crispy potato-topped lamb pies

1 tablespoon olive oil

1 onion, coarsely chopped

750g lamb mince

2½ cups (625ml) beef stock

1 tablespoon chopped rosemary leaves

2 tablespoons Dijon mustard

2 tablespoons honey

2 parsnips, peeled and chopped

1 cup (120g) fresh or frozen peas

500g floury (starchy) potatoes, peeled and thinly sliced

30g butter, melted, for brushing

Preheat oven to 190°C (375°F). Heat a non-stick frying pan over medium heat. Add oil and onion and cook for 4 minutes or until soft. Add the lamb mince and cook, stirring, for 5 minutes or until browned. Add stock, rosemary, mustard, honey and parsnip and simmer for 20-25 minutes or until the mince and parsnip are tender and the mixture has reduced. Stir in peas and spoon mixture into 4 x 1½-cup (375ml) capacity pie dishes. Place potato on top and brush with butter. Bake the pies in the oven for 35–40 minutes or until potato is crisp. Freeze for up to 3 months. **SERVES 2 NOW & 2 LATER.**

veal osso bucco with herbs

8 x 200g slices veal shin with bone in

plain (all-purpose) flour, for dusting

1½ tablespoons olive oil

12 baby or spring onions, peeled and trimmed

1 litre chicken stock

1 cup (250ml) dry white wine

2 celeriac (celery root), peeled and chopped

600g potatoes, peeled and chopped

4 bay leaves

8 sprigs lemon thyme

4 sprigs sage

4 large pieces lemon rind

sea salt and cracked black pepper

Preheat oven to 160°C (320°F). Dust the veal in flour. Heat oil in a heavy-based baking dish over high heat. Add the veal and cook for 3-4 minutes each side or until well browned. Add onions, stock, wine, celeriac, potatoes, bay leaves, thyme, sage, lemon rind, salt and pepper. Cover tightly and bake for 2 hours or until the veal is tender. To freeze, place half the veal and vegetables in an airtight container, seal and freeze for up to 3 months. **SERVES 2 NOW & 2 LATER.**

PORCINI MUSHROOM & CHICKEN PIE

LAMB SHANKS WITH PRESERVED LEMON

porcini mushroom & chicken pie

16g dried porcini mushrooms (G)
¼ cup (60ml) boiling water
2 tablespoons olive oil
1 onion, sliced
1 clove garlic, crushed
3 x 140g chicken thigh fillets, cubed
2 tablespoons plain (all-purpose) flour
1 cup (250ml) chicken stock
¾ cup (90g) fresh or frozen peas
½ cup flatleaf parsley leaves, roughly chopped
6 sheets (25cm x 25cm) store-bought puff pastry, thawed
lightly beaten egg, for brushing
onion slices, for topping
rocket (arugula) leaves, to serve

Preheat oven to 200°C (390°F). Place porcini in a small bowl, cover with boiling water and allow to stand for 10 minutes. Drain the porcini, reserve soaking liquid and chop porcini finely. Heat oil in a large non-stick frying pan over medium heat, add onion and garlic and cook, stirring, for 2 minutes or until onion softens slightly. Add chicken, cook 2 minutes more, stir in flour then add porcini, reserved soaking liquid and stock and cook for 10 minutes, or until sauce thickens. Stir in peas and parsley, remove from heat and set mixture aside to cool. Cut 12 pastry rectangles measuring 10cm x 12cm. Place 6 pastry rectangles on baking trays lined with non-stick baking paper and divide chicken mixture among them. Brush edges of the pastry with egg, cover with remaining pastry rectangles and press edges to seal. Top with onion slices, brush pies with egg and bake for 18 minutes or until the pastry is puffed and golden. Serve with rocket leaves. To freeze, wrap the pies in baking paper, then plastic wrap and aluminium foil to seal. Freeze for up to 3 months. **SERVES 2 NOW & 4 LATER.**

The best method for avoiding freezer burn and those unsightly dried-out edges on food that has been improperly stored in the freezer is to make sure you enclose the food properly before freezing it. When freezing pies, be sure to wrap them in a layer of baking paper, then aluminium foil and finally seal in a layer of plastic wrap.

lamb shanks with preserved lemon

1 tablespoon olive oil
8 French-trimmed lamb shanks (G)
2 onions, cut into wedges
3 sprigs rosemary
6 sprigs lemon thyme
2 tablespoons shredded preserved lemon rind (G)
1 litre chicken stock
1 cup (250ml) dry white wine
2 tablespoons Dijon mustard
4 potatoes, peeled and halved
4 carrots, peeled and halved
sea salt and cracked black pepper
caper gremolata
⅓ cup flatleaf parsley leaves
1 tablespoon capers, rinsed and drained
2 teaspoons finely grated lemon rind

To make caper gremolata, place parsley, capers and lemon rind on a chopping board and chop to a fine mixture. Preheat oven to 180°C (355°F). Heat a heavy-based baking dish over medium–high heat. Add the oil and shanks and cook, turning occasionally until browned. Add onion, rosemary, thyme and preserved lemon and cook for 2 minutes. Add stock, wine and mustard, cover tightly and bake for 1 hour. Add potatoes, carrots, salt and pepper, cover and cook for 40 minutes. Remove cover and cook for an extra 30 minutes, or until lamb is tender. Serve with gremolata. Freeze for up to 3 months. **SERVES 2 NOW & 2 LATER.**

roast tomato & mint soup

2.5kg ripe tomatoes, halved
⅓ cup oregano leaves
sea salt and cracked black pepper
olive oil, for drizzling
2 cups (500ml) chicken or vegetable stock
2 tablespoons balsamic vinegar
1 tablespoon sugar
1 cup chopped mint

Preheat oven to 180°C (355°F). Place the tomatoes cut side up in a baking dish lined with non-stick baking paper. Sprinkle with oregano, salt and pepper; drizzle with oil. Roast for 30 minutes or until soft and slightly browned. Place in a food processor and blend until smooth. Place mixture into a saucepan over medium heat. Add stock, vinegar and sugar and simmer for 4 minutes. Stir through mint. Freeze for up to 3 months. **SERVES 2 NOW & 2 LATER.**

ROAST TOMATO & MINT SOUP

smoked salmon potato cakes

600g potatoes, peeled and chopped
250g hot smoked salmon, flaked
2 tablespoons roughly chopped dill leaves
2 teaspoons grated horseradish (G)
1 tablespoon finely grated lemon rind
1 egg
sea salt and cracked black pepper
plain (all-purpose) flour, for dusting
1 tablespoon butter
1 tablespoon vegetable oil
lemon mayo (recipe, page 116), to serve
rocket (arugula) leaves and lime cheeks, to serve

Cook potatoes in a pan of salted boiling water for 10–15 minutes or until tender. Drain and mash. Place in a bowl with salmon, dill, horseradish, lemon rind, egg, salt and pepper and mix to combine. Shape mixture into 8 patties, dust with flour. Heat butter and oil in a large non-stick frying pan over medium-high heat, add salmon cakes and cook for 2 minutes each side or until golden. Serve the patties with lemon mayo, rocket and lime cheeks. Freeze for up to three months. **SERVES 2 NOW & 2 LATER**.

spinach & ricotta cannelloni

500g frozen spinach, thawed and drained
1kg fresh ricotta
2 eggs
½ cup coarsely chopped flatleaf parsley leaves
¾ cup (60g) finely grated parmesan
sea salt and cracked black pepper
12 fresh lasagne sheets, cut to 11cm x 15cm rectangles
1 litre tomato passata (G)
1 cup (250ml) water
3 cloves garlic, crushed
½ cup chopped basil leaves
1 cup (100g) grated mozzarella

Preheat oven to 180°C (355°F). Combine spinach, ricotta, eggs, parsley, ½ cup (40g) of the parmesan, salt and pepper in a bowl and mix well. Divide ricotta mixture between lasagne sheets and roll to enclose. Place in a greased dish. Combine passata, water, garlic and basil and pour over the cannelloni rolls. Cover with foil and bake for 35 minutes, remove foil and sprinkle with combined mozzarella and remaining parmesan. Bake for 20 minutes or until cheese is melted. Freeze for up to 3 months. **SERVES 2 NOW & 4 LATER**.

pumpkin & coconut soup

1.5 litres chicken or vegetable stock
1 tablespoon fish sauce
4 kaffir lime leaves, bruised
1.5kg pumpkin, peeled, seeded and coarsely chopped
1¼ cups (310ml) coconut milk
½ cup coriander (cilantro) leaves
lime wedges and chopped chives, to serve
finely sliced long red chilli, to serve

Place a large pot over medium heat. Add stock, fish sauce, lime leaves and pumpkin, bring to the boil and cook for 8–10 minutes, or until pumpkin is tender. Remove from heat and remove and discard the lime leaves. Place pumpkin mixture in a blender and process, in batches, until smooth. Return the pumpkin mixture to saucepan over medium heat, add coconut milk and heat, without boiling, for 3 minutes or until soup is heated through. Divide soup between bowls, top with coriander and serve with lime wedges, chives and chilli. Place the remaining soup in an airtight container and freeze for up to 3 months. **SERVES 2 NOW & 4 LATER**.

mint & rosemary lamb meatballs

2 cloves garlic, crushed
1kg lamb mince
2 tablespoons finely chopped mint leaves
1 tablespoon finely chopped rosemary leaves
2 tablespoons Dijon mustard
2 tablespoons honey
200g feta, crumbled
2 tablespoons olive oil
1 cup (250ml) beef stock
3 cups (750ml) tomato passata (G)
¼ cup finely chopped oregano leaves

Place garlic, mince, mint, rosemary, mustard, honey and feta in a bowl and mix well. Roll tablespoonfuls of the mixture into balls. Heat 1 tablespoon of the oil in a large non-stick frying pan over medium–high heat, add half the meatballs and cook for 3 minutes, or until brown on all sides. Add remaining oil and brown remaining meatballs. Reduce heat to medium, return meatballs to pan with stock and passata and simmer for 12–15 minutes, or until meatballs are cooked through. Add the oregano and cook for 1 minute more. Freeze for up to 3 months. **SERVES 2 NOW & 4 LATER**.

CHEATS 6.

nibbles

Having friends around for drinks or dinner doesn't mean you have to declare a holiday to get ready for them. This selection of simple snacks and starters can be put together on the spin of a stiletto, leaving plenty of time for important matters such as organising the right glasses and napkins, fresh flowers in vases and music to suit the occasion and the guest list.

martini olives

RIGHT: Combine 1 cup (160g) green or black olives, ½ cup (125ml) gin, 2 teaspoons lime zest and 6 juniper berries in a glass jar or bowl. Cover and marinate for 1 hour or overnight. To serve, place in a bowl or on a plate with a raised edge with a little of the martini marinade so the olives are lightly coated in the gin mixture.

bocconcini in chilli oil

BELOW: Cut 6 small red chillies lengthways and combine with ½ cup (125ml) olive oil in a small saucepan over low heat. Bring to a simmer and cook gently for 10 minutes. Remove from heat and set aside to cool. Place 220g baby or cherry bocconcini in a bowl and pour over the cooled chilli oil. Allow cheese to marinate for 1 hour or overnight.

It's amazing how a simple combination of flavours and a little time can transform a bland or familiar ingredient into an unexpected treat. Chilli, garlic, vinegar and herbs inject zesty notes.

marinated feta

ABOVE: Place ⅓ cup (80ml) olive oil in a saucepan over very low heat. Add 4 sliced garlic cloves, 4 teaspoons shredded lemon rind and ¼ teaspoon cracked black pepper and warm for 2 minutes then set aside to cool. Place 400g creamy feta onto a serving plate with ½ cup mint leaves. Pour over the cooled oil and marinate for 10 minutes to overnight. Serve with crackers, fresh bread or crispbread.

balsamic caramelised artichoke hearts

LEFT: Cut 8 artichoke hearts in brine in half and pat dry. Place ½ cup (125ml) balsamic vinegar and ¼ cup (55g) sugar into a medium non-stick frying pan over medium heat and cook for 3–4 minutes or until thickened. Add the artichokes and toss to coat. Sprinkle with sea salt and cracked black pepper and serve with slices of crusty bread.

garlic & white bean dip

RIGHT: Heat 2 tablespoons olive oil in a saucepan over low heat. Add 4 finely sliced garlic cloves and cook for 1–2 minutes, or until fragrant. Set aside. Place a 400g can of drained and rinsed white (cannellini) beans into a food processor and process until roughly chopped. Add half the garlic oil plus ¼ cup (60ml) extra olive oil, 1 tablespoon lemon juice and sea salt and process until smooth. Serve with remaining garlic oil.

chickpea patties

BELOW: Place a 400g can of drained and rinsed chickpeas (garbanzos) into a food processor with 1 teaspoon of ground cumin and 1 teaspoon ground coriander (cilantro), 1 egg, ⅓ cup flatleaf parsley leaves, sea salt flakes and cracked black pepper. Process until the mixture is coarsely chopped. Shape the mixture into patties. Cook patties in a little hot olive oil until golden. Serve with store-bought tzatziki (G), flatbread and lemon wedges. **MAKES 4 PATTIES.**

The fabulous flavours of the Mediterranean inspired these dips, spreads and patties. They're made in minutes but become glam party fare when served with flatbread or crackers.

yoghurt & feta dip

ABOVE: Combine 1 cup (280g) natural yoghurt with 200g crumbled soft feta, 1 crushed garlic clove, 2 teaspoons lemon juice and 2 tablespoons finely chopped mint leaves. Serve with thin slices of Turkish bread. This dip can be made up to 24 hours in advance and stored, covered, in the refrigerator until just before serving time.

instant hummus

LEFT: Place a 400g can of drained and rinsed chickpeas (garbanzos) or white (cannellini) beans into a blender. Add ¼ cup (70g) of tahini paste (G), 1 crushed garlic clove, 1 tablespoon lemon juice, sea salt and ¼ cup (60ml) water. Blend until smooth. To serve, drizzle with olive oil and sprinkle with paprika, sumac or ground chilli.

crispy duck pies

RIGHT: Remove 300g of meat from a store-bought Chinese barbecued duck and chop finely. Add 2 tablespoons hoisin sauce, 1 tablespoon plum sauce and 2 finely chopped green onions (scallions). Place spoonfuls of the duck mixture on 12 gow gee wrappers and brush the edges with beaten eggwhite. Top with another wrapper and press to seal. Brush with vegetable oil, place on a lined baking tray and bake in a preheated 180°C (355°F) oven for 8 minutes or until crisp. Serve with plum sauce. **MAKES 12.**

mini pork hoisin rolls

BELOW: Place a non-stick frying pan over high heat. Brush a 240g pork fillet with sesame oil and sprinkle with 1 tablespoon Chinese five-spice powder and sea salt. Cook for 2 minutes each side or until well browned. Cover, reduce the temperature to low and cook for 5–7 minutes or until cooked through Slice the pork and divide among 10 warmed store-bought Chinese pancakes or crepes. Top with sliced green onion (scallion) and hoisin sauce, roll up. Serve with cucumber ribbons and extra hoisin. **MAKES 10.**

Asian cultures have perfected the bite-sized snack. From Chinese dim sum to Thai street fare, there's always a flavour-packed morsel at hand to kick-start the palate and keep hunger at bay.

thai wonton cups

ABOVE: Brush 12 wonton wrappers with oil, sprinkle with sesame seeds and press into small muffin tins. Bake in a preheated 180°C (355°F) oven for 7 minutes or until golden brown. In a frying pan warm 50g brown sugar, 1 tablespoon lime juice and 2 tablespoons each of fish sauce and water. Add 1 cup (160g) shredded cooked chicken and warm through. Stir in ¼ cup coriander (cilantro) leaves, 2 shredded lime leaves and 1 chopped long red chilli. Spoon into wonton cups. **MAKES 12.**

wasabi beans

LEFT: Cook a 400g packet of frozen soy beans in their pods (edamame) in salted boiling water for 6–8 minutes or until tender, drain. Place 30g butter, 2–3 teaspoons wasabi paste, 1 teaspoon water and sea salt into a large non-stick frying pan over medium heat and cook until butter is melted. Toss in the soy beans to coat and serve warm in small bowls or cups. To eat squeeze the beans from the pods. **SERVES 4.**

INSTANT DESSERTS

Is it just coincidence that stressed spelled backwards is desserts? A sensational sweet finale can dispel all manner of pressures, including a hard day at work and an early start in the morning. So restore your sanity and spoil your family and friends with these simple treats that can be flipped together with minimum effort for maximum impact.

ESPRESSO TIRAMISU

FLOURLESS CHOCOLATE CAKE

espresso tiramisu

⅓ cup (80ml) strong black coffee
⅓ cup (80ml) coffee liqueur
2 tablespoons brown sugar
1 cup (250g) mascarpone
¼ cup (60ml) cream
½ teaspoon vanilla extract
2 tablespoons brown sugar, extra
8 small (or 4 halved) store-bought sponge finger biscuits

Place coffee, liqueur and sugar in a saucepan over medium heat and simmer for 5-6 minutes or until thickened slightly. Pour into a bowl and refrigerate until cold. Whisk together mascarpone, cream, vanilla and extra sugar. Place 2 biscuits on each plate and spoon over some of the coffee syrup. Top with large spoonfuls of the mascarpone mixture and then the remaining biscuits. Drizzle with remaining coffee syrup. SERVES 2.

When a cake tin size is recommended we always measure the bottom of the pan. Even if there's a measurement stamped onto the tin, remeasure to check its accuracy. The best cream for whipping is single, or pouring, cream, which has a butter fat content of 20–30 per cent. It whips to a light, airy consistency, perfect for serving with cakes.

flourless chocolate cake

350g quality dark chocolate, chopped
185g unsalted butter, chopped
6 eggs
1 cup (220g) brown sugar
¼ cup (60ml) hazelnut liqueur
1 cup (100g) ground hazelnuts
hazelnut cream
300ml cream
¼ cup (60ml) hazelnut liqueur, extra

Preheat oven to 170°C (340°F). Line the base and sides of a 22cm springform pan with non-stick baking paper. Place chocolate and butter into a saucepan over low heat and stir until melted. Place eggs, sugar, liqueur and hazelnuts into a bowl and whisk to combine. Add chocolate mixture and whisk until smooth. Spoon mixture into tin and cover with aluminium foil. Bake for 40 minutes. Remove foil and cool cake in tin then refrigerate until cold. To make hazelnut cream, place the cream and liqueur in a bowl and beat with electric beaters or a whisk until soft peaks form. Cover and refrigerate until just before serving. Serve with hazelnut cream. SERVES 12.

raspberry cake

⅓ cup (50g) plain (all-purpose) flour
⅔ cup (80g) almond meal (ground almonds)
1 cup (160g) icing (confectioner's) sugar
90g butter, melted
3 eggwhites, lightly beaten
1 teaspoon vanilla extract
1 cup frozen or fresh raspberries
extra raspberries and whipped cream, to serve

Preheat oven to 160°C (320°F). Combine flour, almond meal, icing sugar, butter, eggwhites and vanilla in a bowl and mix until smooth. Fold half the berries through and spoon into a greased 18cm round cake tin that has been lined with non-stick baking paper. Sprinkle the remaining berries on top of the mixture and bake for 35-40 minutes or until cooked when tested with a skewer. Serve the cake warm with whipped cream with extra raspberries folded through. SERVES 6.

RASPBERRY CAKE

cheat's sticky toffee puddings

100g dates, chopped
²/₃ cup (160ml) boiling water
¼ teaspoon bicarbonate of soda (baking soda)
30g butter, softened
½ cup (110g) brown sugar
1 egg
²/₃ cup (150g) self-raising (self-rising) flour
thick cream or ice-cream and extra brown sugar, to serve

Preheat oven to 160°C (320°F). Place dates, boiling water
and bicarbonate of soda in a heatproof bowl and set aside
for 10 minutes. Process the date mixture until smooth. Add
butter, sugar, egg and flour and process until smooth. Pour
mixture into 4 well-greased 1-cup (250ml) ovenproof bowls or
small pudding basins and place on a baking tray. Bake for
25 minutes or until puddings are cooked when tested with a
skewer. Invert puddings onto serving plates and serve with
thick cream sprinkled with extra brown sugar. **SERVES 4.**

caramelised hazelnut parfait

½ cup (70g) roasted hazelnut kernels
1 teaspoon hazelnut-flavoured liqueur
1 tablespoon brown sugar
½ cup (125ml) hazelnut-flavoured liqueur, extra
ice-cream, to serve

Preheat oven to 160°C (320°F). Place hazelnuts and liqueur
in a small bowl and toss well to coat. Place sugar in a bowl,
add hazelnuts and toss to coat. Place sugar-coated hazelnuts
on a baking tray lined with non-stick baking paper and spread
out to form a single layer. Place in oven and bake for 12 minutes,
or until sugar bubbles and caramelises. Remove from oven and
cool slightly. Place extra liqueur in a small saucepan over high
heat and boil rapidly for 8 minutes, or until the mixture is thick
and syrupy and reduced by half. Allow to cool slightly. To serve,
place scoops of ice-cream in bowls, top with caramelised nuts
and liqueur syrup. **SERVES 2.**

chocolate truffle mousse

1¼ cups (310ml) cream
125g dark chocolate, chopped
2 egg yolks
30g butter

Place cream in a saucepan over medium heat and heat until almost boiling. Remove from heat, add chocolate, egg yolks and butter and stir until smooth. Chill mixture until cold. Place mixture in the bowl of an electric mixer, beat until light and creamy — try not to overbeat or it will be grainy. Spoon the mousse into small glasses and serve with thin store-bought butter biscuits. **SERVES 2.**

chocolate fondant puddings

200g dark chocolate, melted
60g butter, chopped
2 eggs
2 tablespoons plain (all-purpose) flour
⅓ cup (60g) brown sugar
cream or ice-cream, to serve

Preheat oven to 180°C (355°F). Place chocolate, butter, eggs, flour and sugar into a food processor and process until smooth. Spoon into 2 x 1-cup (250ml) capacity greased ramekins. Bake for 18–20 minutes or until puddings are cooked on the outside and just set in the middle. Stand for 10 minutes before turning out onto plates and serve with cream or ice-cream. **SERVES 2.**

UPSIDE-DOWN PLUM CAKE

MOCHA TRUFFLES

upside-down plum cake

50g butter, melted
¼ cup (55g) brown sugar
2 plums, stones removed and sliced
butter cake
80g butter
⅓ cup (75g) brown sugar, extra
1 egg
½ cup (75g) self-raising (self-rising) flour
½ teaspoon vanilla extract
whipped cream, to serve

Preheat oven to 160°C (320°F). Pour the melted butter into the base of an 18cm round cake tin. Sprinkle with sugar and arrange the plum slices over the sugar. To make the cake, place butter, sugar, egg, flour and vanilla into the bowl of an electric mixer and beat for 4 minutes or until light and smooth. Spoon the mixture over plums and bake for 35 minutes or until cake is cooked when tested with a skewer. Invert the cake onto a plate and serve with whipped cream. **SERVES 4.**

You could use any firm fruit such as apples or pears for this cake. Turn the cake out as soon as it comes out of the oven, as the toffee topping sets very quickly and it could become stuck in the tin. Don't stress if it does, however, as you can pop the cake back in the oven for a few minutes and the toffee will melt again.

mocha truffles

1 tablespoon instant coffee granules
1 teaspoon boiling water
400g dark chocolate
⅔ cup (160ml) cream
cocoa powder, for dusting

Combine coffee and water in a cup and stir until coffee is dissolved. Place the coffee mixture, chocolate and cream in a saucepan over low heat and stir until chocolate melts and mixture is smooth. Line a 14cm x 14cm x 6cm cake tin with non-stick baking paper, pour in chocolate mixture and refrigerate 2–3 hours or until set. Cut into squares and dust with cocoa. **MAKES 24.**

chocolate-raspberry meringue mess

100g dark chocolate, chopped
¾ cup (180ml) cream
2 store-bought meringues
½ cup (125ml) cream, extra
150g raspberries

Place the chocolate and cream in a saucepan over low heat and stir until smooth, place in a bowl and set aside. Roughly crush the meringues. Place some of the meringue into serving glasses. Whip extra cream until soft peaks form. Spoon some of the chocolate mixture over crushed meringue, top with a few raspberries then a little whipped cream. Repeat layers. **SERVES 2.**

CHOCOLATE-RASPBERRY MERINGUE MESS

coconut rice with seared mango

2 cups (330g) cooked rice
1 cup (250ml) coconut milk
1 vanilla bean, split and seeds removed
⅓ cup (75g) sugar
½ cup (125ml) water
2 mangoes
caster (superfine) sugar, for sprinkling

Combine rice, coconut milk, vanilla seeds, sugar and water in a medium saucepan over medium heat and cook, stirring occasionally, for 8 minutes, or until the sugar is dissolved and the rice mixture is slightly thickened. Remove from heat and refrigerate until cold. Cut two cheeks from each mango and sprinkle cut side with sugar. Heat a medium non-stick frying pan over high heat, place the cheeks, sugared side down, in the pan and cook for 30 seconds or until the sugar is melted. Divide the coconut rice among serving bowls and serve with the seared mango cheeks. **SERVES 4**.

coconut-chocolate tarts

¾ cup (60g) desiccated coconut
⅓ cup (75g) caster (superfine) sugar
1 eggwhite
chocolate ganache filling
140g dark chocolate, chopped
⅔ cup (160ml) cream

Preheat the oven to 140°C (280°F). Combine coconut, sugar and eggwhite in a bowl and mix well. Line a baking sheet with non-stick baking paper and place 6 greased 7.5cm diameter egg rings on the sheet. Press the coconut mixture into the egg rings to make an even shell on the base and sides. Bake for 20 minutes or until the shells are lightly browned. Allow to cool slightly before removing from the rings and filling with chocolate filling. To make chocolate ganache filling, combine chocolate and cream in a small saucepan over low heat and cook, stirring, until chocolate melts. Remove from heat and cool before pouring into the shells. Refrigerate for 1 hour or until filling sets. **MAKES 6**.

stonefruit with golden topping

4 stone fruit, halved
1¼ cups (310ml) dessert wine
1 vanilla bean, split, seeds scraped
1 cinnamon stick
100g plain butter cake, crumbled
40g butter, melted

Preheat oven to 180°C (355°F). Place stone fruit, cut-side down, in a baking dish, add wine, vanilla and cinnamon stick. Bake for 15 minutes, turn fruit and bake for a further 15 minutes. Combine crumbled cake and melted butter, sprinkle over fruit and bake for 10–15 minutes or until crumbs are crispy and golden. **SERVES 4**.

banana maple puddings

2 tablespoons caster (superfine) sugar
2 tablespoons maple syrup
²/₃ cup mashed banana
50g butter, melted
1 egg
½ cup (75g) self-raising (self-rising) flour
thick cream, to serve
extra maple syrup, to serve

Preheat oven to 170°C (340°F). Place the sugar, maple syrup, banana, butter, egg and flour into a small bowl and mix until combined. Spoon mixture into 2 greased 1-cup (250ml) capacity ramekins and bake for 30–35 minutes or until cooked when tested with a skewer. Serve puddings warm with a dollop of thick cream and extra maple syrup. **SERVES 2**.

PASSIONFRUIT MERINGUES

CRUNCHY BAKED APPLE STACKS

passionfruit meringues

150ml eggwhites (you will need 4 eggs)
1 cup (220g) caster (superfine) sugar
2 tablespoons passionfruit pulp (approx 2 passionfruit)
extra whipped cream, to serve
extra passionfruit pulp, to serve

Preheat oven to 120°C (250°F). Place eggwhites in the bowl of an electric mixer and beat until soft peaks form. Gradually add the sugar and beat until sugar dissolves and the mixture is thick and glossy. Fold in passionfruit pulp. Line a baking tray with non-stick baking paper and spoon 2 tablespoonfuls of the meringue mixture onto tray. Bake for 25 minutes. Turn off oven and allow meringues to cool in the oven for 2 hours. Serve with whipped cream with passionfruit pulp stirred through. MAKES 20.

There is no great secret to making meringue beyond getting the proportions right. This ratio of eggwhite to sugar makes what I consider the perfect meringue: crunchy on the outside with a firm marshmallow texture in the centre. The only other trick is to cool meringues slowly in a turned-off oven, which will stop them collapsing.

crunchy baked apple stacks

½ cup (80g) blanched almonds, finely chopped
¼ cup (55g) sugar
pinch ground cinnamon
15g soft butter
2 red apples, cored and thickly sliced
double (heavy) cream, to serve

Preheat oven to 180°C (355°F). Place almonds, sugar, cinnamon and butter in a small bowl. Line a baking tray with non-stick baking paper. Place 2 slices of apple on the tray and top each slice with a spoonful of the almond mixture. Repeat with remaining almond mixture and apple slices. Bake stacks for 25 minutes or until apple is just soft. Serve with a dollop of double cream. SERVES 2.

instant peach custard pies

2 peaches, stones removed and thinly sliced
2 egg yolks
1 egg, extra
1¼ cups (310ml) cream
⅓ cup (75g) caster (superfine) sugar
1 teaspoon vanilla extract

Preheat oven to 160°C (320°F). Layer peaches in 4 x 1¼-cup (310ml) capacity greased ovenproof pie dishes. Place the egg yolks, extra egg, cream, sugar and vanilla in a blender or food processor and blend until smooth. Divide the egg mixture among the dishes. Bake for 18–20 minutes or until the custards are just firm. Serve warm. SERVES 4.

INSTANT PEACH CUSTARD PIES

maple apple tarte tatin

25g butter
¼ cup (60ml) maple syrup
1 apple, cored and sliced
2 sheets (25cm x 25cm) store-bought puff pastry, thawed

Preheat oven to 180°CC (355°F). Place the butter in an 18cm non-stick frying pan with an ovenproof handle. Place pan over medium heat until butter melts. Add maple syrup, arrange the apple in overlapping slices over the base of the pan and cook for 5–6 minutes or until just soft. Remove from heat and set aside. Cut 2 x 19cm circles of pastry to fit inside the pan and place on top of each other on the apple. Bake for 30–35 minutes or until the pastry is puffed and golden. Allow to stand for 2 minutes, then invert onto a plate. You can serve the tarte tatin warm or at room temperature. **SERVES 4**.

berry bread & butter puddings

butter, for spreading
4 slices of bread or brioche
1 cup frozen raspberries or blueberries
3 eggs
1½ cups (375ml) milk
⅓ cup (70g) caster (superfine) sugar
1 teaspoon vanilla extract
vanilla ice-cream, to serve

Preheat oven to 160°C (320°F). Butter bread and cut each slice into 8 strips. Divide the bread between 4 greased 1-cup (250ml) capacity ramekins. Sprinkle with berries. Whisk together eggs, milk, sugar and vanilla, pour over bread and stand for 2 minutes. Bake for 35–40 minutes or until puddings are just cooked in the centre. Serve warm with vanilla ice-cream. **SERVES 4**.

macaroon-filled pears

2 firm brown pears, halved lengthways
2 eggwhites
⅓ cup (75g) caster (superfine) sugar
¾ cup (60g) shredded coconut
caramel ice-cream, to serve

Preheat oven to 180°C (355°F). Remove core and hard fibres
from pears, trim bases so they sit flat. Place the eggwhites in a
small bowl and beat with electric beaters until soft peaks form.
Gradually add in sugar, beating until sugar dissolves and firm
peaks form. Fold through coconut and divide mixture among
the pear halves. Bake in oven for 25 minutes or until macaroon
mixture is firm and lightly browned. Serve with a large scoop of
caramel ice-cream. **SERVES 4**.

lemon & coconut impossible pies

½ cup (110g) caster (superfine) sugar
2 tablespoons self-raising (self-rising) flour
⅓ cup (25g) desiccated coconut
½ teaspoon baking powder
1 teaspoon finely grated lemon rind
¼ cup (60ml) lemon juice
15g butter, melted
⅓ cup (80ml) milk
1 egg

Preheat oven to 180°C (355°F). Place the sugar, flour, coconut
and baking powder in a bowl and mix to combine. In a separate
bowl, combine lemon rind, juice, butter, milk and egg and stir
to mix well. Pour the lemon mixture into the dry ingredients and
stir until well mixed. Pour into 2 x 1-cup (250ml) capacity greased
ovenproof pie or gratin dishes. Bake for 18–20 minutes or until
the tops are golden brown and there is a thick sauce underneath.
Serve the pies warm. **SERVES 2**.

CHEATS 7.

- - - - - - - - - - - - - - - - - - - -

sweet treats

- - - - - - - - - - - - - - - - - - - -

Let's face it, there's really no occasion when
the world's going to stop rotating on its axis
because you don't serve something sweet at the
end of a meal. But there are times when you
could end up in a spin if you don't have a sugar
fix to serve with coffee or for dessert. These sweet
sensations fill the bill when it's hard to tell
the difference between needs and wants.

honeycomb

RIGHT: Place 1 cup (220g) of sugar, ⅓ cup (80ml) honey and 60g butter in a large saucepan and stir until the sugar dissolves. Bring mixture to the boil and cook for 2 minutes or until the syrup is a golden colour. Remove from the heat and stir through 2 teaspoons of bicarbonate of soda (baking soda). The mixture will foam. Pour into a greased 20cm-square tin. Allow to cool and break into pieces. Store in an airtight jar. Serve with coffee. **MAKES 25 BITE-SIZED PIECES.**

little s'mores

BELOW: Place 6 small chocolate chip or chocolate cookies on a baking tray lined with non-stick baking paper. Place a small piece of dark chocolate on each cookie and top with half a marshmallow. Bake the cookies in a preheated 160°C (320°F) oven for 3 minutes or until the marshmallow is just starting to brown. Top with another cookie and serve immediately. Stand back and wait for them to call for s'more. **MAKES 6.**

The intense flavour of coffee demands a robust companion. Chocolate makes a serendipitous match, but toffee treats come a close second. The only tricky part will be stopping at one.

brandy brownie truffles

ABOVE: Place 1 cup (180g) crumbled store-bought, good quality brownie in a bowl and sprinkle with 2 teaspoons brandy. Roll heaped teaspoons of the mixture into balls and roll in cocoa powder to coat, then refrigerate until firm. You could also roll these truffles in icing (confectioner's) sugar, powdered drinking chocolate, flaked almonds or toasted coconut if you prefer. **MAKES 12.**

chocolate almond crackle

LEFT: Place 1 cup (140g) toasted slivered almonds on a greased baking tray and press to flatten out to one layer. Place 1½ cups (330g) sugar and ⅓ cup (80ml) water in a saucepan over high heat. Cook without stirring for 8–10 minutes or until mixture is a golden colour. Pour toffee over the almonds and allow to set. Spread 150g of melted dark chocolate over the almond toffee and allow to set in the refrigerator. Break into large pieces and serve with coffee. **MAKES 20 PIECES.**

caramelised wonton stacks

RIGHT: Preheat oven to 180°C (355°F). Place 6 wonton wrappers on a baking tray lined with non-stick baking paper. Brush wontons with 15g melted butter and sprinkle with 1 tablespoon brown sugar combined with ½ teaspoon of ground cinnamon. Bake for 7–8 minutes or until golden and crisp. Cool wontons and store in an airtight container until needed. To serve, layer the wontons with large scoops of your favourite flavour of ice-cream or sorbet. **SERVES 2.**

chocolate stars

BELOW: Using a cookie cutter, cut 16 star shapes from 2 sheets (25cm x 25cm) thawed store-bought puff pastry. Place an 8g piece of chocolate in the centre of 8 of the stars, brush the outsides with lightly beaten egg, top with remaining stars and press the edges together to seal. Brush the stars with egg and sprinkle with caster (superfine) sugar. Bake in a preheated 180°C (355°F) oven for 15 minutes or until golden. Serve with coffee or hot chocolate. **MAKES 8 STARS.**

Sweet pastries transport the diner into deep comfort territory and ready rolled store-bought pastry makes the passage even smoother. If the occasion calls for light and fresh it's hard to beat fruit 'n' fizz.

apple & raspberry turnovers

ABOVE: Cut 12 x 9cm rounds from 2 thawed sheets (25cm x 25cm) store-bought puff pastry with a fluted edged cutter. Top half the pastry rounds with a slice of cored red or green apple and ½ teaspoon of raspberry jam. Brush the pastry edges with lightly beaten egg, cover with remaining pastry and press to seal. Brush with the egg, sprinkle with caster (superfine) sugar and bake in a preheated 180°C (355°F) oven for 15 minutes or until golden. **MAKES 6.**

moscato fruit

LEFT: Place a selection of sliced seasonal fruit in small serving glasses. In summer you can choose from peaches, nectarines, apricots, plums and berries; and in winter, pears, figs or just-thawed frozen berries. Top each glass with well-chilled Moscato wine just before serving. Substitute a pink sparkling wine or Champagne for the Moscato if desired. **MAKES 2.**

chocolate espresso sundae

RIGHT: Combine 75g dark chocolate, 1 tablespoon strong espresso coffee (or 1 tablespoon coffee granules) and ⅓ cup (80ml) cream in a small saucepan over low heat and stir until smooth. Remove from heat and allow to cool. Place large scoops of vanilla ice-cream in glasses or small serving bowls, pour over topping and top with chocolate-coated coffee beans to serve. **SERVES 4.**

nougat sundae

BELOW: Place large scoops of vanilla ice-cream in 4 tall serving glasses. Divide 300g roughly chopped store bought pistachio, almond, rosewater or chocolate nougat among the glasses. You could also drizzle over your favourite nut-flavoured liqueur, a crunchy topping of crushed store-bought amaretti or biscotti or finely chopped nuts. **SERVES 4.**

The combination of ice-cream and toppings is simplicity itself, a real bonus for cooks on the go. Start with the best quality ice-cream you can find and you'll soon be serving up a sublime sweet sensation.

turkish delight sundae

ABOVE: Place large scoops of vanilla ice-cream into 4 bowls and divide 250g roughly chopped store-bought rosewater Turkish delight between the bowls. Sprinkle with ½ cup (70g) chopped pistachios to serve. You could also sprinkle over some roughly chopped white or dark chocolate. **SERVES 4.**

rum 'n' raisin sundae

LEFT: Combine ½ cup (70g) raisins, 1 cup (250ml) rum and 1 cup (220g) brown sugar in a small saucepan. Place over high heat and simmer rapidly for 8–10 minutes or until syrupy. Remove from heat and cool. Place scoops of vanilla or caramel-flavoured ice-cream in 4 bowls and spoon over rum-infused raisins to serve. **SERVES 4.**

GLOSSARY

We have our wonderful multicultural society
to thank for the many ingredients that have
enlivened our table in recent years. I'm mindful,
however, that not all of you will have access
to speciality food stores, so wherever possible,
we've tried to source most of the ingredients from
supermarkets. If you're unsure of, or unable to
obtain, a particular item, this glossary will help.

almond meal

Also known as ground almonds, almond meal is available from most supermarkets. Used instead of, or as well as, flour in cakes and desserts. Make your own by processing whole skinned almonds to a fine meal in a food processor or blender (125g almonds will give 1 cup almond meal). To remove the skins from almonds, soak in boiling water, then using your fingers, slip the skins off.

arborio rice

Risotto rice with a short, plump-looking grain. It has surface starch which creates a cream with the stock when cooked to al dente. Substitute with carnaroli, roma, baldo, padano, vialone or Calriso rice.

asian greens

These leafy green vegetables from the brassica family are now becoming widely available. We love their versatility and speed of preparation – they can be poached, braised, steamed or added to soups and stir-fries.

BOK CHOY: A mildly flavoured green vegetable, also known as Chinese chard or Chinese white cabbage. Baby bok choy can be cooked whole after washing. If using the larger type, separate the leaves and trim the white stalks. Limit the cooking time so it stays green and crisp.

BROCCOLINI: A cross between gai larn (Chinese broccoli) and broccoli, this green vegetable has long, thin stems and small florets. Sold in bunches, it can be substituted for broccoli.

CHOY SUM: Also known as Chinese flowering cabbage, this green vegetable has small yellow flowers. The green leaves and slender stems are steamed or lightly cooked in soups and stir-fries.

GAI LARN: Also known as Chinese broccoli or Chinese kale, gai larn is a leafy vegetable with dark green leaves, small white flowers and stout stems.

balsamic vinegar

A rich, dark colour and a sweet, mellow, almost caramel flavour distinguish balsamic vinegars from other wine vinegars. Made from trebbiano grapes in Modena, Italy, it is aged for 5 to 30 years, or more. The older the balsamic, the better (and more expensive) and the less you'll need to use. Cheaper ones may need to be balanced with some sugar. It can't be used as a substitute for regular vinegar.

blanching

A cooking method used to slightly soften the texture, heighten the colour and enhance the flavour of food such as vegetables. Plunge the ingredient briefly into boiling unsalted water, then remove and refresh under cold water. Drain well before using in salads or as a garnish.

brioche

A sweet, buttery French yeast bread made in loaf or bun form. Traditionally dunked in coffee at breakfast. Available from speciality bread and cake stores and some supermarkets, brioche makes great bread and butter pudding.

burghul

Cereal made from wheat that has been steamed or par-boiled, dried, debranned and crushed into grains. A popular ingredient in Turkish, Middle Eastern, Indian and Mediterranean cuisines, burghul should be covered with boiling water for 15–20 minutes to reconstitute before use.

butter

Unless stated otherwise in a recipe, butter should be at room temperature for cooking. It should not be half-melted or too soft to handle, but should still have some "give" when pressed. When using butter for pastry, it should be cold and chopped into small pieces so that it can be evenly distributed through the flour. Salted butter has a longer shelf life, which makes it preferable for some people.

butter (lima) beans

A large, plump white bean also known as a Lima bean. It goes well in soups, stews and salads. Available from delicatessens and supermarkets either canned or in dried form.

buttermilk

Originally the name given to the slightly tangy liquid which was left over when cream was separated from milk, these days buttermilk is manufactured by adding cultures to low- or no-fat milk. Buttermilk is used in sauces, marinades, dressings and baking.

capers

Capers are the small, green flower buds of the caper bush. Available packed either in brine or salt. Use salt-packed capers when possible, as the texture is firmer and the flavour superior. Before use, rinse thoroughly, drain and pat dry.

caperberries

Caperberries come from the same bush as caper buds, but are its oblong, unripe fruit. About the same size as a small grape, caperberries are also milder in flavour and slightly less acidic than the buds. Before use, rinse thoroughly, drain and pat dry.

celeriac

A root vegetable (also called celery root) with white flesh and a mild celery flavour. It is available in winter from supermarkets and greengrocers. Use in salads and soups or roast it with meats.

cheese

A nutritious food made by curdling the milk of cows, goats, sheep and buffalo using rennet and acidic cultures. Some cheeses have pronounced flavours from moulds on the outer rind or throughout the whole product.

BLUE: The distinctive veins and flavour of blue cheeses are achieved by adding a cultured mould. Most have a crumbly texture and acidic taste, which becomes rounded and more mellow with age.

FETA: Made from goat's, sheep's or cow's milk, feta is a salty, crumbly cheese, which is frequently stored in brine to extend its shelf life.

GOAT'S: Goat's milk has a tart flavour, so cheese made from it, sometimes labelled chèvre, has a sharp, slightly acidic taste. Immature goat's cheese is milder and creamier than mature cheese and is sometimes labelled curd.

HALOUMI: Firm white Cypriot cheese made from sheep's milk. It has a stringy texture and is usually sold in brine. Available from delicatessens and some supermarkets. Holds its shape during grilling and frying, so is ideal for kebabs.

MASCARPONE: A fresh Italian triple-cream, curd-style cheese. It has a similar consistency to thick (double) cream and is often used in the same way. Available in tubs from speciality food stores, delicatessens and supermarkets, it's used in sauces and desserts such as tiramisu.

MOZZARELLA & BOCCONCINI: Italian in origin, mozzarella is the mild cheese of pizza, lasagne and tomato salads. It's made by cutting and spinning (or stringing) the curd to achieve a smooth, elastic consistency. The most-prized variety is made from buffalo milk. Bocconcini are small, bite-sized balls of mozzarella.

PARMESAN: Italy's favourite hard, granular cheese is made from cow's milk. Parmigiano reggiano is the "Rolls Royce" variety, made under strict guidelines in the Emilia-Romagna region and aged for an average of two years. Grana padano mainly comes from Lombardy and is aged for 15 months.

RICOTTA: A creamy, finely grained white cheese. Ricotta means "recooked" in Italian, a reference to the way the cheese is produced by heating the whey left over from making other cheese varieties. It's fresh and creamy and low in fat.

chervil

A herb relative of parsley with a slightly aniseed flavour and aroma.

chilli jam

Thai condiment made from ginger, chilli, garlic and shrimp paste used in soups and stir-fries. It goes well with roasted meats, egg dishes and cheese.

chinese five-spice powder

A blend of cinnamon, Sichuan pepper, star anise, clove and fennel seeds. Available at Asian food stores and supermarkets.

chorizo

Firm, spicy, coarse-textured Spanish pork sausage seasoned with pepper, paprika and chillies. Available from some butchers and most delicatessens.

coconut milk

A milky sweet white liquid made by soaking grated fresh coconut flesh or desiccated coconut in warm water and squeezing through muslin or cheesecloth to extract the liquid. Available in cans or freeze-dried from supermarkets, coconut milk should not be confused with coconut juice, which is a clear liquid found inside young coconuts.

cornichons

Small, young cucumbers pickled in vinegar or brine and often with dill.

couscous

The name given to both the national dish of Algeria, Tunisia and Morocco and the tiny grains of flour-coated semolina that make it. Available from supermarkets.

cream

The fat content determines the names of the different types of cream and the uses for which they are ideal.

SINGLE OR POURING CREAM: Has a butter fat content of 20–30 per cent. It is the type of cream most commonly used for making ice-cream, panna cotta and custard. It can be whipped to a light and airy consistency and served on the side.

THICKENED CREAM: Not to be mistaken for heavy or double cream, this is single or pouring cream that has had a vegetable gum added to stabilise it. The gum makes the cream a little thicker and easier to whip. It's ideal for desserts or for topping cakes and pavlovas.

HEAVY OR DOUBLE CREAM: Has a butter fat content of 40–50 per cent. It is sometimes called pure cream and is usually served on the side.

eggs

The standard egg size used in this book is 60g. It is very important to use the right size eggs for a recipe, as this will affect the outcome of baked goods. The correct volume is especially important when using eggwhites to make meringues. You should use eggs at room temperature for baking so always remember to remove them from the refrigerator about 30 minutes before you begin cooking.

fennel

With a mild aniseed flavour and crisp texture, fennel bulb is ideal for salads or roasted with meat and fish. It is available from supermarkets and greengrocers.

fish sauce

An amber-coloured liquid drained from salted, fermented fish and used to add flavour to Thai and Vietnamese dishes. Available from supermarkets and Asian food stores, it's often labelled "nam pla".

french-trimmed lamb shanks

A meat cut is said to be French-trimmed or Frenched when all meat and fat is removed from one end of the bone. It makes the cut easier to pick up and more attractive for presentation.

harissa

A North African condiment, harissa is a hot red paste made from chilli, garlic and spices including coriander, caraway and cumin. May also contain tomato. Available in jars and tubes from supermarkets and speciality food stores, harissa enlivens tagines and couscous dishes and can be added to dressings and sauces for an instant flavour kick.

hoisin sauce

A thick, sweet Chinese sauce made from fermented soybeans, sugar, salt and red rice. Used as a dipping sauce or marinade and as the sauce for Peking duck, hoisin is available in supermarkets.

horseradish

A pungent root vegetable that releases mustard oil when cut or grated. It oxidises quickly, so use immediately after cutting or cover with water or vinegar. Available fresh from greengrocers or grated in jars from supermarkets.

hummus

Popular dip of the Middle East made by blending cooked chickpeas (garbanzos) with tahini, garlic and lemon juice. Available in tubs from supermarkets.

kaffir lime leaves

Fragrant leaves with a distinctive, double-leaf structure, used crushed or shredded in Thai dishes. Available fresh or dried from Asian food stores.

lemongrass

A tall, lemon-scented grass used in Asian cooking, and particularly in Thai dishes. Peel away the outer leaves and chop the tender root-end finely, or add in large pieces during cooking and remove before serving. Available from Asian food stores and some greengrocers.

maple syrup

A sweetener made from the sap of the maple tree. Be sure to use pure maple syrup rather than imitation or pancake syrup, which is made from corn syrup flavoured with maple and lacks the flavour of the real thing.

miso paste

A traditional Japanese ingredient produced by fermenting rice, barley or soybeans, with salt and fungus to a thick paste. Used for sauces and spreads, pickling vegetables or meats, and mixing with dashi soup stock to serve as miso soup. Available from supermarkets and Asian food stores.

noodles

Like pasta, keep a supply of dried noodles in the pantry for last-minute meals. Fresh noodles will keep in the fridge for a week. Available from supermarkets and Asian food stores

BEAN THREAD: Also called mung bean vermicelli, cellophane or glass noodles, these noodles are very thin and almost transparent. Soak them in boiling water and drain well to prepare for use.

CHINESE WHEAT: Available dried and fresh in a variety of thicknesses. Fresh noodles need to be soaked in hot water or cooked in boiling water. Dried noodles should be boiled before use.

FRESH RICE: Available in a variety of thicknesses, including thin, thick and rolled. Use noodles which are a few days old at most, soak in hot water for 1 minute, and drain well to prepare for use.

DRIED RICE STICK: Fine, dry noodles that are common in Southeast Asian cooking. Depending on their thickness, rice noodles need only be boiled briefly, or soaked in hot water until pliable.

nori

Thin sheets of dried, vitamin-packed seaweed used in Japanese-style dishes and to wrap sushi. Available in packets from supermarkets and Asian food stores.

olives

Black olives are more mature and less salty than the green variety. Choose firm olives with good colour and a pronounced fruity taste.

LIGURIAN/WILD OLIVES: Usually labelled or sold as Ligurian olives, wild olives are uncultivated and grow close to the ground in clusters. This small variety of olive can range in colour from pale mustard to dark purple and black. The thin flesh has a nutty flavour that makes them a great substitute for peanuts. Niçoise olives are similar in size as well as flavour.

KALAMATA OLIVES: Of Greek origin, the large Kalamata olives have an intense flavour, which makes them the ideal choice for Greek salads. They are sometimes sold split to better absorb the flavour of the oil or vinegar in which they are stored.

olive oil

Olive oil is graded according to its flavour, aroma and acidity. Extra virgin is the highest quality oil; it contains no more than 1 per cent acid. Virgin is the next best; it contains 1.5 per cent or less acid and may have a slightly fruitier taste than extra virgin. Bottles labelled "olive oil" contain a combination of refined and unrefined virgin olive oil. Light olive oil is the least pure in quality and intensity of flavour; it is not lower in fat. Colours vary from deep green through to gold and very light yellow.

oyster sauce

A viscous dark brown sauce commonly used in Asian stir-fries, soups and hotpots, oyster sauce is made from oysters, brine and flavour enhancers, which are boiled until reduced to a thick, caramelised, flavour-packed sauce.

pancetta

A cured and rolled Italian-style meat that is like prosciutto but less salty and with a softer texture. It's sold in chunks or thinly sliced and can be eaten uncooked or used in pasta sauces and risottos.

paprika

Spice made from ground, dried capsicum. Originally from Hungary, it comes in mild (sweet), smoky and a hot Spanish version. Adds flavour and vibrant colour to meat and rice dishes.

pastry

Make your own or use one of the many store-bought varieties.

PUFF: This pastry is time-consuming and quite difficult to make, so many cooks opt to use store-bought puff pastry. It can be bought in blocks from pâtisseries or bought in both block and sheet forms from supermarkets. You may need to layer several sheets of puff pastry together to make a thicker crown.

SHORTCRUST: A savoury or sweet pastry that is available ready-made in blocks and frozen sheets. Keep a supply for last-minute pies or make your own pastry:

2 cups (300g) plain (all-purpose) flour
145g butter
2–3 tablespoons iced water

Process the flour and butter in a food processor until the mixture resembles fine breadcrumbs. While the motor is running, add enough iced water to form a smooth dough. Knead very lightly then wrap the dough in plastic wrap and refrigerate for 30 minutes. When ready to use, roll out on lightly floured surface to 3mm thick. This recipe makes 350g, which will line a 25cm pie dish or tart tin.

pickled ginger (gari)

Japanese in origin, pickled ginger is made by preserving thin slices of young ginger in sweetened vinegar. Gari is often served with sushi as it is thought to cleanse the palate between bites. Buy it at Asian food stores and supermarkets.

polenta

Used extensively in northern Italy, this corn meal is cooked in simmering water until it has a porridge-like consistency. In this form it is enriched with butter or cheese and served with meat dishes. Otherwise it is left to cool, cut into squares and grilled, fried or baked.

porcini mushrooms

Available fresh in Europe and the UK and sold dried elsewhere, including Australia and the US. They have an almost meaty texture and earthy taste. Soak dried porcini mushrooms before using, and use the soaking liquid if desired. Frozen porcinis are becoming more readily available. Like the dried variety, they're available from delicatessens and speciality food stores.

preserved lemon

Preserved lemons are rubbed with salt, packed in jars, covered with lemon juice and left for about four weeks. Remove the flesh and chop the rind for use in cooking. Available from delicatessens and speciality food stores.

prosciutto

Italian ham that's been salted and dried for up to two years. The paper-thin slices are eaten raw or used to lend their distinctive flavour to braises and other cooked dishes. Often used to wrap figs or melon as part of an antipasto platter.

red curry paste

Buy good-quality pastes in jars from Asian food stores or the supermarket. When trying a new brand, it is a good idea to add a little at a time to test the heat as the chilli intensity can vary significantly from brand to brand.

red curry paste recipe

3 small red chillies
3 cloves garlic, peeled
1 stalk lemongrass, chopped
4 green onions (scallions), chopped
1 teaspoon shrimp paste
2 teaspoons brown sugar
3 kaffir lime leaves, sliced
1 teaspoon finely grated lemon rind
1 teaspoon grated ginger
½ teaspoon tamarind concentrate
2–3 tablespoons peanut oil

Place all the ingredients except the oil in the bowl of a small food processor or spice grinder. With the motor running, slowly add the oil and process until you have a smooth paste. Refrigerate in an airtight container for up to 2 weeks. Makes approximately 1 cup.

rice flour

A fine flour made from ground white rice. Used as a thickening agent, in baking and to coat foods when cooking Asian dishes, particularly those needing a crispy finish. Buy from supermarkets.

rice vinegar

Made from fermenting rice or rice wine, rice vinegar is milder and sweeter than vinegars made by oxidising distilled alcohol or wine made from grapes. Rice wine vinegar is available in white (colourless to pale yellow), black and red varieties from Asian food stores and some supermarkets.

shaoxing wine

Similar to dry sherry, Shaoxing or Chinese cooking wine is a blend of glutinous rice, millet, a special yeast and the local spring waters of Shao Hsing, where it is made, in northern China. It is sold in Asian supermarkets, often labelled "shao hsing".

shrimp paste

Also called blachan, this strong-smelling paste is made from salted and fermented dried shrimps pounded with salt. Used in Southeast Asian dishes. Keep sealed in the fridge and fry before using. Available from Asian food stores.

sichuan peppercorns

Dried berries with a spicy, tongue-tingling effect that are sold whole. Toast in a hot, dry frying pan until fragrant before crushing or grinding for use in Chinese and other Asian recipes.

smoked salmon

Salmon cured in a smokehouse. Cold smoking at less than 30°C delivers a moist, delicately flavoured result. Hot-smoked salmon is cooked while smoking, so is drier and firmer in texture than the cold-smoked product. It also has a stronger flavour, so if you are substituting it for cold-smoked salmon use a smaller quantity.

sponge finger biscuits

Sweet and light Italian finger-shaped biscuits, also known as savoiardi. Great for desserts such as tiramisu because they absorb other flavours and soften well, yet at the same time maintain their shape. These biscuits are available in large and small versions from delicatessens and most supermarkets.

star anise

Small, brown seed-cluster that is shaped like a star. It has a strong aniseed flavour that can be used whole or ground in sweet and savoury dishes. Available from supermarkets and speciality food stores.

sugar

Extracted as crystals from the juice of the sugar cane plant or beet, sugar is a sweetener, flavour enhancer, bulking agent and preservative.

BROWN SUGAR: Processed with molasses. It comes in differing shades of brown, according to the quantity of molasses added, which varies between countries. This also affects the taste of the sugar, and therefore the end product. Brown sugar is sometimes called light brown sugar. You can substitute dark brown sugar for more intense flavour.

CASTER (SUPERFINE): Gives baked products a light texture and crumb, which is important for many cakes and light desserts such as meringues.

ICING (CONFECTIONER'S): Regular granulated sugar ground to a very fine powder. It often clumps together and needs to be sieved before using. Use pure icing sugar not icing sugar mixture, which contains cornflour (cornstarch) and needs more liquid.

REGULAR (GRANULATED OR WHITE): Regular sugar is used in baking when a light texture is not crucial. The crystals are large, so you need to beat, add liquids or heat regular sugar to dissolve it.

sumac

Dried berries of a flowering plant are ground to produce an acidic, purple powder popular in the Middle East.

sweet potato

Long, tuberous root available in white- and orange-fleshed varieties. The orange sweet potato, also known as kumara, is sweeter and moister than the white. Both varieties can be roasted, boiled or mashed. Although different from the yam, they can be cooked in a similar manner.

tahini

A thick paste made from ground sesame seeds. Used in Middle Eastern cooking, it is available in jars and cans from supermarkets and health food shops.

tapenade

Paste made by blending olives, capers, garlic and anchovies with oil. Served as a dip with crackers, or spread on bruschetta and pizzas, it makes a good marinade and partner for cold meat.

tins

Aluminium (aluminum) tins are fine but stainless steel will last longer and won't warp or buckle. Always measure tin widths at the base.

MUFFIN: The standard sizes are a 12-hole tin, each hole with ½-cup (125ml) capacity, or a 6-hole tin, each hole with 1 cup (250ml) capacity. Mini-muffin tins have a capacity of 1½ tablespoons. Non-stick tins make for easy removal, or line with paper patty cases.

ROUND: The standard sizes for round springform tins are 18cm, 20cm, 22cm and 24cm. The 20cm and 24cm tins are must-haves.

SPRINGFORM: The standard sizes for round tins are 18cm, 20cm, 22cm and 24cm. The 20cm and 24cm round tins are the must-have members of the range.

SQUARE: The standard sizes for square tins are 18cm, 20cm, 22cm and 24cm. If you have a recipe for a cake cooked in a round tin and you want to use a square tin, the general rule is to subtract 2cm from the size of the tin. You would need a 20cm square tin for a recipe calling for a 22cm round cake tin.

tofu

Literally translated as "bean curd", tofu is a high-protein food popular across Asia. Made by coagulating the milk of soy beans, and pressing the curd into blocks, tofu comes in several grades according to the amount of moisture which has been removed. Silken tofu is the softest, with a custard or junket-like texture. Soft tofu is slightly firmer with the texture of raw meat, while dried or firm tofu has the texture of, and cuts like, a semi-hard cheese such as haloumi or paneer. Usually sold packed in water from the refrigerated section of supermarkets and Asian food stores. You can also buy packaged deep-fried tofu.

tomato passata

Italian for "passed", passata is made by removing the skins and seeds from ripe tomatoes and passing the flesh through a sieve to make a thick, rich, pulpy tomato purée. Sugo is made from crushed tomatoes so it has a little more texture than passata. Both are available in bottles from supermarkets and are essential to the Italian table.

tzatziki

Greek dip made from thick natural yoghurt, garlic and chopped or grated cucumber, sometimes with dill added. Available in supermarkets, it can also be used as a sauce for grilled meat and seafood or served as an accompaniment to savoury pastries.

vanilla beans

These cured pods from the vanilla orchid are used whole, and often split and the tiny seeds scraped into the mixture, to infuse flavour into custard and cream-based recipes. If unavailable, substitute 1 vanilla bean with 1 teaspoon pure vanilla extract (a dark, thick liquid – not essence).

vanilla extract

For a pure vanilla taste, use a good-quality vanilla extract, not an essence or imitation flavour, or use a vanilla bean.

vine leaves

Also called grape leaves, as they come from the grape vine, they are used as an edible wrapping for foods and are the wrapper for the rice-based appetisers known as dolmades or dolmas. Sold in some supermarkets and delicatessens.

wasabi

Wasabi is a very hot Japanese horseradish paste used in making sushi and as a condiment. Available from Asian food stores and supermarkets.

white (cannellini) beans

These small, kidney-shaped beans are available from supermarkets either canned or in dried form. Dried beans need to be soaked overnight in water before cooking.

wonton wrappers

Chinese in origin, these square thin sheets of dough are available fresh or frozen. They can be steamed or fried. Fill them with meat and vegetables to make dumplings for soup or use as a crunchy base for nibbles, or deep-fried and sprinkled with sugar for dessert.

MEASURES & CONVERSIONS

The language of preparing and sharing good
food may be international but, from time
to time, one country's cups and measures can
become lost in translation from another's.
We hope these pages eliminate all possible
points of confusion so that no matter where
you live, you'll be able to enjoy using our easy
recipes by following these simple guidelines.

GLOBAL MEASURES

Measures vary from Europe to the US & even from Australia to NZ.

metric & imperial

Measuring cups and spoons may vary slightly from one country to another, but the difference is generally not sufficient to affect a recipe. All cup and spoon measures are level. An Australian measuring cup holds 250ml (8 fl oz).

One Australian metric teaspoon holds 5ml, one Australian tablespoon holds 20ml (four teaspoons). In North America, New Zealand and the UK they use 15ml (three-teaspoon) tablespoons.

When measuring liquid ingredients remember that 1 American pint contains 500ml (16 fl oz), but 1 Imperial pint contains 600ml (20fl oz).

When measuring dry ingredients, add the ingredient loosely to the cup and level with a knife. Don't tap or shake to compact the ingredient unless the recipe requests "firmly packed".

LIQUIDS & SOLIDS

Measuring cups & spoons & a set of scales are great assets in the kitchen.

liquids

cup	metric	imperial
⅛ cup	30ml	1 fl oz
¼ cup	60ml	2 fl oz
⅓ cup	80ml	2½ fl oz
½ cup	125ml	4 fl oz
⅔ cup	160ml	5 fl oz
¾ cup	180ml	6 fl oz
1 cup	250ml	8 fl oz
2 cups	500ml	16 fl oz
2¼ cups	600ml	20 fl oz
4 cups	1 litre	32 fl oz

solids

metric	imperial
20g	½ oz
60g	2 oz
125g	4 oz
180g	6 oz
250g	8 oz
500g	16 oz (1lb)
1kg	32 oz (2lb)

MADE TO MEASURE

Equivalents for metric & imperial measures & ingredient names.

millimetres to inches

metric	imperial
3mm	⅛ inches
6mm	¼ inch
1cm	½ inch
2.5cm	1 inch
5cm	2 inches
18cm	7 inches
20cm	8 inches
23cm	9 inches
25cm	10 inches
30cm	12 inches

ingredient equivalents

bicarbonate soda	baking soda
capsicum	bell pepper
caster sugar	superfine sugar
celeriac	celery root
chickpeas	garbanzos
coriander	cilantro
cos lettuce	romaine lettuce
corn flour	cornstarch
eggplant	aubergine
green onion	scallion
plain flour	all-purpose flour
rocket	arugula
self-raising flour	self-rising flour
silverbeet	Swiss chard
snow pea	mange tout
zucchini	courgette

OVEN TEMPERATURE

Setting the oven to the right temperature can be critical when making baked goods.

celsius to farenheit

celsius	farenheit
120°C	250°F
140°C	280°F
160°C	320°F
180°C	355°F
190°C	375°F
200°C	390°F
220°C	400°F

electric to gas

celsius	gas
110°C	¼
130°C	½
140°C	1
150°C	2
170°C	3
180°C	4
190°C	5
200°C	6
220°C	7
230°C	8
240°C	9
250°C	10

BUTTER & EGGS

Let 'fresh is best' be your mantra when it comes to selecting dairy goods.

butter

For baking we generally use unsalted butter as it lends a sweeter flavour. Either way the impact is minimal. One American stick of butter is 125g (4 oz).

eggs

Unless otherwise indicated we use large (60g) chicken eggs. To preserve freshness, store eggs in the refrigerator in the carton they are sold in. Use only the freshest eggs in recipes that use raw or barely cooked eggs such as mayonnaise or dressings. Be extra cautious if there is a salmonella problem in your community, particularly in food that is to be served to children, the elderly or pregnant women.

COMMON INGREDIENTS

Here are some simple weight conversions for cups of common ingredients.

common ingredients

almond meal
1 cup ¦ 120g

brown sugar
1 cup ¦ 220g

white sugar
1 cup ¦ 220g

caster (superfine) sugar
1 cup ¦ 220g

icing (confectioner's) sugar
1 cup ¦ 150g

plain or self-raising (self-rising) flour
1 cup ¦ 150g

fresh breadcrumbs
1 cup ¦ 70g

finely grated parmesan cheese
1 cup ¦ 80g

uncooked rice
1 cup ¦ 200g

cooked rice
1 cup ¦ 165g

uncooked couscous
1 cup ¦ 200g

cooked, shredded chicken, pork or beef
1 cup ¦ 160g

olives
1 cup ¦ 150g

INDEX

You know it's in this book, but you just can't find the recipe you're after? Stress no more, this index is designed to be as helpful as it can possibly be. As well as listing recipes by name, we've also made multiple entries so you can find the recipe you're looking for under its key ingredients, or according to its broader category, whether it's cakes, salads or patties.

THANK YOU

A book is a very detailed and painstaking process and only comes together with much help from some extremely talented people. Con Poulos is my work soul mate, calm, kind and generous with his spirit, time, creativity and patience. Thank you for your amazing contribution to this book. When Clare Stephens said she would come on board to design the book I thought all of my Christmases had come at once and I wasn't wrong. Her gorgeous designs make every page shine. To our wise and witty editor Kirsty McKenzie, thanks for being the glue that sticks everything together. Thanks also to Ali Irvine for all your hard work and hilarity. Eternal gratitude to design guru Sarah Kavanagh for her watchful eye. Thanks to the dh mag food team: Justine, Steve, Jane and Lucy and to Petrina Frost, dh brand legend and true supporter. Also to Shona Martyn at HarperCollins for her exuberant enthusiasm. And last, but by no means least, thanks to my boys big and small, Bill, Angus and Tom, who keep me smiling and make my world a happier place.

Prop credits: Royal Doulton – Gordon Ramsay by Royal Doulton, Jasper Conran at Wedgwood, Kelly Hoppen at Wedgwood, Dibbern Pure from Beclau and Chefs' Warehouse.